William Jessup University
Library
333 Sunset Blvd.
Rocklin, Ca 95765

FOR BETTER CHURCH MEETINGS

25801

FOR BETTER CHURCH MEETINGS

Jerold W. Apps

SAN JOSE BIBLE COLLEGE LIBRARY
790 S. 12th St. P.O. Box 1090
San Jose, California 95108

AUGSBURG PUBLISHING HOUSE
MINNEAPOLIS, MINNESOTA

ACKNOWLEDGMENTS

Dr. Lee Swan, former president of the Midvale Community Lutheran Church, and Pastor Stan Klyve, Senior Pastor, were of great help in critically reviewing the manuscript and suggesting improvements. Nancy Trager has my thanks for typing various drafts of the manuscript.

IDEAS FOR BETTER CHURCH MEETINGS

Copyright © 1975 Augsburg Publishing House

Library of Congress Catalog Card No. 75-2842

International Standard Book No. 0-8066-1487-0

Quotations from *Adult Education Procedures* by Paul Bergevin, Dwight Morris, and Robert M. Smith © 1963, The Seabury Press, Inc. Used by permission. Excerpts appearing on pages 94-96 of this publication are reprinted by permission of and copyrighted 1966 and 1972 by Minnesota Mining and Manufacturing Company.

All rights reserved. No part of this book may be used or reproduced in any manner whatsoever without written permission except in the case of brief quotations embodied in critical articles and reviews. For information address Augsburg Publishing House, 426 South Fifth Street, Minneapolis, Minnesota 55415.

Manufactured in the United States of America.

Contents

Introduction	7
1. Is This Meeting Necessary?	10
2. Selecting Committees	15
3. How to Plan for a Meeting	18
4. Decisions	33
5. The Decision-Making Process	41
6. Understanding Group Members	57
7. The Group Leader	69
8. How to Involve Members in Meetings	77
9. Visuals Aid Understanding	90
10. The Congregational Business Meeting	98
11. Be a Better Speaker	108
12. How Are We Doing?	120
Notes	126

Introduction

No matter how large or small your church, it has meetings. People meet to worship together each Sunday, educational meetings are conducted for both children and adults, the men and the women of the church meet, the youth meet, the church council and the various planning committees meet.

The church's very life depends on people getting together to worship, to share, to plan, and to make decisions.

The emphasis of this book is on helping to improve meetings where decisions are made and problems solved. The focus will be on three types of church meetings:

1. *Committee meetings*—both standing and temporary committees. Examples of *standing committees* include: worship, personnel, education, social action, buildings and grounds, stewardship, and finance. *Temporary committees* might be: a call committee to select a new pastor, a constitution committee to revise the present constitution, or a committee appointed to plan a church's 100th anniversary. Standing committees operate on a continuing basis; temporary committees are appointed to accomplish a specific task and are then dismissed.

2. *Council or board meetings*—the policy and decision makers for the church.

3. *Business meetings*—such as the congregational annual meeting. The business meeting is a special kind of

meeting and will be treated separately, with its own chapter, though many of the principles discussed for the other types of meetings apply.

One difference between the business meeting and the other decision-making meetings is size. When a group is larger than 20 or 25 people, approaches differ from those used with smaller decision-making groups.

A close relationship often exists between study groups and decision-making groups. Indeed sometimes study groups become decision-making groups.

For example, a group may meet to discuss and learn about various worship forms. As a result of their study, the group may become a decision-making group and recommend to the church council that the present worship form used in the church be changed. The group was not organized to make decisions (advocate a new worship form), yet after study the group felt it important to take some action based on their study.

Or the study group on worship forms may recommend that the church's worship and music committee—assuming there is such a committee—should look at alternative worship forms and make recommendations for changes in how worship is presently done.

The three types of meetings—committee meetings, council or board meetings, and business meetings—have in common the purpose of involving people to make decisions and solve problems.

In my work with various kinds of church groups, I often hear both pastors' and members complaining about meetings. I've heard:

"They're boring. I'd rather do almost anything than go to some meetings."

"Most meetings I go to don't have a purpose. We get together and talk and talk, but nobody seems to know what we're trying to accomplish. One person says our purpose is one thing, someone else says it's something else."

"We spent all that time meeting. I bet one person by himself could have come up with a better decision than we did—and a lot quicker too."

"Meetings—all they're held for is to rubber stamp the pastor's ideas, or an idea the chairman has. Why should I bother to come?"

You've likely heard some things about meetings that you could add to this list. People are saying that meetings:

1. are boring;
2. have no purpose or a confused purpose;
3. often result in no decisions or poor decisions;
4. are rubber stamps for someone else's decisions.

We could wring our hands and say how terrible. But we could also try to improve the situation. Before there can be improvement, there must be a commitment to improve. And that commitment must come from committee moderators,* pastors, and particularly from those who attend and participate in meetings, in non-designated leadership roles. This book is written for everyone who wants to improve church meetings.

---

* Throughout this book the designated leader of a committee will be referred to as a *moderator*, who may be either male or female.

1

Is This Meeting Necessary?

Do several people have to get together for just about every decision that is made in your church? Does every problem get passed along to either some standing committee, the church council, or a special committee? If that's the situation at your church, it's not unusual. But have you ever thought that maybe your church didn't need to have so many committee meetings, that the council didn't need to meet quite as often or as long, and that some special committees need not have been appointed at all?

Decisions can be made without calling a group together. I know what you're thinking. Churches in a democratic society should be run in a democratic way. And to be run in a democratic way, people must be involved in making all the decisions.

I am not suggesting churches not be democratic. Indeed many decisions must be made by the people. But not all of them. There are many decisions the congregation wants to have made, and they don't care much when they are not involved. Unfortunately, in some congregations, some members don't want to become involved in the *important* decisions either. But that's another issue.

If you accept that not every decision needs group action, the question then is, how do you decide when a group should become involved? Start by looking at the nature of the problem to be solved and the kind of decision to be made.

There are two dimensions to every decision: (1) quality and (2) acceptance. *Quality* means that the decision is a good one, the best one possible for the given situation. Quality decisions are usually based on intelligence and knowledge. *Acceptance* means that those who must carry out the decision like it. Acceptance of a decision is usually based on participation and involvement.

A quality decision is based on facts and good thinking. Acceptance of a decision is more difficult because it is based on feelings, what people like and dislike, or something they can't even put into words. You'll hear people say, "That idea seems right to me." The feeling may be backed up with facts and good thinking, but then again it may not.

What's important though, is that *more decisions fail because they lack acceptance than because they lack quality*. Think about that. How many great ideas never came to life because they were not accepted? I've seen some excellent curriculum guides produced by national church offices. They were colorful, they were likely accurate, they had been field-tested with selected church schools around the country. In a word, they had *quality*. But until they were accepted by a congregation's education committee all that quality rested between two covers.

So we can't overlook acceptance when we are dealing with decisions. Indeed, there may be times when we must sacrifice some quality, to get acceptance. As a general rule, a decision of average quality that is accepted is better than a high quality decision that is never implemented. We all want to work for the highest quality decisions possible, but without acceptance we gain nothing.

Now, back to the original question. How do we know when a meeting should be called to make a decision? Maier says there are four problem situations.[1] For two of the situations it's necessary that a group make the decision, for the other two the decision can be made without a group.

Situation 1

The requirement for a high quality decision is important, and acceptance of the decision is not likely to be an issue.

Let's say your church has budgeted some money to buy audiovisual equipment. What's important is that you get the best equipment possible for the money you have. A committee doesn't need to haggle over whether you should buy Kodak, Argus, Bell and Howell, or some other brand. One person, with some advice from an audiovisual expert, can make the decision. Why waste the time of a group? Acceptance is not likely to be a problem. The people want the best equipment they can get for the money. Most groups would have to do the same as an individual—ask for expert outside advice.

Here's another classic example. You're a passenger on a jet plane flying over the Atlantic Ocean. One engine quits. Do you insist that the pilot call a meeting of the passengers to decide what he should do? Or do you accept whatever decision the pilot makes in this emergency situation?

When a decision must be of the highest quality and acceptance of that decision is not likely to be a problem, don't call a meeting.

Situation 2

Quality of the decision isn't an issue, but the need for acceptance is high. This is the opposite of situation one.

Assume your church is building an addition and the architect submits three alternative plans. Each plan will make a serviceable addition. Let's also assume that the addition, no matter which plan is followed, will cost $40,000, which will mean extra giving by the congregation. A committee had better decide which plan the church should follow. Acceptance becomes highly important. The happier people are with the choice, the smoother the whole project will go.

Another example of where high acceptance is important and quality isn't an issue is when you are deciding the fair way to distribute something. Say your church recently remodeled half of its Sunday school rooms. Which teachers should get the remodeled rooms? The quality of teaching will likely be the same, or nearly so, no matter which room the teacher is in. Who gets the remodeled rooms? Let the teachers decide among themselves. If it's their decision, the degree of acceptance will increase many times, compared to an arbitrary assignment of rooms by the superintendent.

A third example is determining the fair way to get something undesirable done. For example, say a church office normally has one of its two secretaries work on Sunday mornings—to answer the phone, be available if there is any kind of emergency, and so on. Each of the two secretaries can do the job equally well. Let the two secretaries work out the schedule of who will work which Sundays. They'll likely be much happier than if the pastor arbitrarily makes the assignment.

Situation 3

Neither quality nor acceptance of the decision are an issue.

For example, supplies for Sunday school such as chalk, crayons, and paper must be purchased. It makes no sense for an education committee to waste time deciding what types of supplies should be ordered. One person, given the responsibility to get the best quality materials for the money available, can do the job. And the education committee can deal with more important issues, where quality and acceptance are important.

Another example. Your church has decided to pave

the parking lot. Assuming that three available contractors will do work of similar quality, one person can select the contractor to do the work better than five can do it.

Situation 4

Problems where the requirements for acceptance and the quality of the decision are both high.

Determining the church budget requires all the facts a committee can accumulate, plus the best thinking it can muster. And the decision for a final budget must be accepted by a majority of the congregation or the giving program will be in trouble.

Selecting a new pastor. A church wants the best person they can hire, but at the same time the congregation must like the person who is suggested.

Establishing schedules for Sunday school. What are the availability of rooms and teachers? How many youngsters of each age are there? What other activities are being planned for Sunday morning? These are facts that must be gathered and carefully considered. But the parents, youngsters, and teachers must accept the decision made or there will be problems. The situation, like the others mentioned above, requires both a high quality decision as well as acceptance.

When should a meeting be called? For situations 2 and 4, when acceptance of the decision is an important question.

How do you know when you should call a group together to make a decision? Analyze each problem situation to determine the importance of decision acceptance.

The remainder of this book will deal with those situations where a meeting should be held, emphasizing some of the techniques for achieving quality decisions and acceptance.

2

Selecting Committees

Members of church councils are usually elected by the congregation. Business meetings are open to the entire congregation. But committees are usually made up of people that are *appointed*. Because committee meetings make up the majority of decision-making meetings in many churches, here are some tips for selecting committee moderators and committee members.

Selecting the Moderator

If a committee is to be appointed, the first step is to think of a moderator. More care should be taken in the selection of the moderator than in selecting any of the members. The role of the moderator or chairman is more than to call and preside at meetings of the committee; his primary function is to lead the group toward the completion of the tasks assigned.

> The chairman [moderator] need not be the person with the most knowledge about the topic at hand, but he should be a person who has the ability to organize the individual members into a working group. He may never have served as a committee chairman before, but it will be to the advantage of the group if he has served on a committee or has had similar experience.
>
> The chairman is chosen for his ability to lead the group. "Idea men" are not always the best chairmen.

> The individual who proposes an idea is not necessarily the best choice for a chairman, but neither should he be disqualified—either to be the chairman or a member of the committee.[1]

In most cases it is not a good idea for the members of a group to select their own moderator. Newly appointed committee members usually do not have enough information about each other or the kind of leadership needed.

Selecting Committee Members

Here are some factors to keep in mind when selecting committee members: [2]

1. Which individuals have an interest in the kinds of activity in which the committee will be engaged?

2. Who in the church has the knowledge and skill, or access to information, needed by the committee?

3. Which persons could benefit most by working on the committee with members who have more experience? Serving on committees is an excellent training ground for future church leaders.

4. Are there individuals who might develop a greater sense of belonging or commitment to the church by working on a given committee? Involvement in an activity creates interest and commitment. Committee work can spark interest in people, because they are making a specific contribution to the church and are being recognized for their contributions.

5. Is a representative committee needed? Representation may be needed in one or more of the following areas: (a) representation by differing opinions or points of view, (b) representation by different occupations, (c) representation by various age levels. Obviously, not all committees need to be representative.

6. Which members have the best access to the resources needed to do the job?

7. Are there some individuals who will work together more compatibly than others? If there are people who have demonstrated their inability or unhappiness in working together, it is usually wise not to place them on the same committee.

8. Does the moderator of the committee have any preferences as to who should be on the committee? Often the moderator will have the names of several people in mind for the committee. Because the moderator has so much responsibility for the functioning of the committee, his suggestions should be encouraged and carefully considered.

What Size Committee?

The purpose of the committee should be the prime consideration when determining how large the committee should be. If it's necessary to have wide representation, then the committee will be larger than if representation isn't an issue. As a rule of thumb, the smaller the committee, the more productive it will be. For example, a committee appointed to revise the church's constitution prior to presenting it to the congregation might have but three members. A committee responsible for evaluating the church's entire educational program must be larger, because it must represent the various dimensions of church education.

3

How to Plan for a Meeting

Before we talk about planning, let's visit a church council meeting. Council president Fred Olson, elected earlier this year, chairs the meeting.

The council members sit in the church lounge talking about the rain. The rain started early that morning and shows no sign of quitting. The meeting was scheduled for 7:00 P.M. It's now 7:30.

"Let's get going Fred. We don't want to be here until midnight like last month. Besides it's a terrible night to be away from home," Robert Johnson suggests. Johnson is a doer, not one to sit around and wait, and besides he has to be at work at the local packing plant by 7:00 A.M.

"Might as well. Looks like Pete and Mary aren't gonna make it tonight. Just too wet I suppose. Let's call this council meeting to order then."

The six council members present stop talking and look toward Fred.

"How about us deciding not to go past 10:30 tonight, Fred," asks George Hayes.

"Doubt we can promise that, George. Lots of things to get done you know. Takes time to get the business done. You all have the minutes of the last meeting. Any corrections or additions? Hearing none the minutes stand approved as printed."

Fred turns to George Hayes, treasurer of the church.

"Well George, how we fixed this month? Still going in the red?"

Hayes distributes a two-page summary of the previous month's financial activities which includes a detailed account of all income and expenses. There are columns comparing what was budgeted, pledged, and spent. Paper rattles as the council members turn the sheets back and forth, trying to understand what the numbers mean.

"About this $30.00 for a new clock. Where did we put the clock?" Leonard Ganser asks.

"In the pastor's study," answers Hayes.

There are questions and answers about the budget that take up most of a half hour. Finally President Olson breaks in, "We've got an insurance man coming in here at 8:00. Let's wind up this budget talk. Do I hear a motion?"

Hayes moves for the adoption of the report and it's passed.

The insurance man appears and Fred introduces him. He's a little man with a quiet voice. The committee members listen attentively to his proposal—at first, that is. He spends an hour describing in detail all facets of the insurance policy he hopes to sell the church. The church's present policy expires January 1. Other than the chairman and the pastor, no one else knew the insurance man was coming to the meeting. Roger Johnson is visibly disturbed. He knows the meeting will drag on until midnight. The meeting's important business, if indeed there is any, hasn't been mentioned yet. Traditionally, the group hasn't had an agenda, so no one knows what will happen. Each member is called on, in rotation, to present whatever business he has to the council.

The president usually calls on the first council member to his right, then goes around the table. If you want something discussed, it's well to sit to the president's right, unless of course you have something that's controversial. If it's controversial, you sit to the president's left.

Chances are the president won't get to you until late in the meeting and everyone will be too worn out to debate your item.

"Any questions on this insurance policy?" Fred asks.

"Sounds like a lot of money to me. I move we do some more checking before we make a decision," George Hayes suggests.

"You've heard the motion. Is there a second?"

The motion is seconded and passed, although no one, except Hayes, sounds very happy about delaying until another meeting. The aye's are weak, but the tradition is that whenever possible the vote on motions should be unanimous.

It's 9:15. In two and a quarter hours the committee has approved the minutes of the last meeting, looked at the treasurer's report, and heard an insurance salesman.

George Hayes is yawning. "Why can't we have coffee at these meetings?" he asks.

"Great idea, George. Why don't you look into getting that done," suggests Fred.

"Yeah, I'll look into it," replies Hayes. He doesn't sound very excited about the idea now that he is asked to do something about it. His interests are primarily with money matters. Investment counseling is his business, and he thinks much of what is discussed at the committee meetings is nonsense.

The room is quiet now. Roger Johnson is nearly asleep. Tom Wildman sits immediately to President Olson's right. Fred will call on him first. Those still awake turn toward Tom hoping his business items will be brief, or even better that he doesn't have any business items.

The late hour often excludes some important business items because council members are reluctant to prolong the meeting. No one has a way of determining what is or isn't important though. Someone with an important item may choose not to present it to save time, while someone else with a trivial item may take a half hour presenting it.

The meeting wears on toward 11:00, and then a very long hour later it's midnight. From 11:00 to 12:00 the council discussed what punishment to give the Boy Scout troup that didn't clean up after their last meeting. Before that the council turned down a request by a sex-education group to use the church for a meeting.

At five minutes after midnight Fred adjourned the meeting and the six council members shuffled toward the door and home. The rain had stopped and there was bright moonlight. One of the council members mutters: "Same as last month. Talk, talk, talk—and where are we? We're at midnight with nothing done. Weather sure has changed, though. Look at that moon."

Fred thinks the meeting has gone quite well. This is his impression of how a council should function. When you talk to him he'll tell you about his concern for some of the council members. "They just don't seem interested in what the council is doing."

Was this meeting planned? No. No one knew what business was to be discussed. Few knew the insurance salesman was coming to the meeting. Much information was shared, but few decisions were made.

A Meeting That Was Planned

Let's visit a committee—the Plainville Women's Club Teacher-of-the-Year Committee. There are eight members. Ruth Johnson, committee moderator, arrives 15 minutes before starting time. She introduces herself to each member as they arrive, and introduces the members to one another. Copies of the agenda and other background information are on the table for each member.

The meeting is scheduled for 1:30 P.M., and Ruth promptly calls the meeting to order at that time. She asks each member to introduce herself and tell the group something about herself. There is a name card in front of each person.

"Let's review the agenda," Ruth says as she opens the meeting. Three items are listed: (1) review last year's outstanding teacher award procedure, (2) review criteria for selecting outstanding teacher, and (3) determine a timetable for the committee's activities.

"There may be other agenda items," Ruth says, "But let's start with these."

Lisa White, who is new on the committee, wants to know more about last year's selection procedure. "I know we selected Grace Holt from Plainville High as our outstanding teacher. But I've heard some complaints about that choice. Somebody told me the selection committee did a terrible job. Kids don't like Grace Holt, yet our club gave her an outstanding teacher award. How was she selected? How many candidates were there? What criteria were used?"

"Good questions, Lisa," Ruth says. "In front of you is a description of the procedure we used last year. Let's all look at it and then talk about how the procedure can be improved."

This is the way the committee progressed. Ruth has thought about and planned for this meeting. She knows what needs to be accomplished and leads the committee toward its goals.

Planning a Meeting

The contrast between these two meetings is great. And much of the difference is due to the planning that was done prior to the meeting. The question is, how do you plan for a meeting? Here are some things that should be done before a group meets. Some are done before every meeting of a group. Others are done only before a group meets for the first time.

1. Study the situation.
2. Determine the specific purpose for the meeting.

3. Plan the agenda.
4. Prepare introductory remarks.
5. Make necessary arrangements.
6. Decide on methods and equipment.

Most of these items must be done by the moderator, but this doesn't mean that the participants in a meeting need not prepare before attending. As we discuss the items listed above, you'll see that several of them apply to the participants as well as to the moderator.

I. Study the Situation

GROUP STATUS. What is the status of your group? Is your group one that existed for some time, such as a standing committee, or the church council? Or is the group a temporary one that will meet a few times to accomplish a specific task and then disband?

Some temporary groups try to become permanent.

> It has been observed that once groups are organized and function over a period of time, there is a tendency for them to be self-perpetuating. That is, even after their charge has been fulfilled, they often want to continue meeting; consequently, they will create new tasks for themselves. Sometimes they continue to meet because it has not been made clear that they should disband when the job is finished. Therefore, as soon as the committee has completed its task, or if for some reason the organization decides that the committee should function no longer, it should be definitely discharged and each committee member notified.[1]

A group which has existed for several years will function differently from one recently appointed. With the established group, you must consider its history. Who are the continuing members? What has been previously accomplished by the group? What procedures has the group followed in its operations?

BROAD FUNCTIONS. What is the function of your group? Decision-making groups generally have one of the following three functions (some will be concerned with more than one):

1. *To plan and take action.* Examples are a couple's club committee that plans and conducts programs, or an adult education committee that plans curriculum and also staffs the adult education activities.

2. *To make policy decisions that someone else will carry out.* The church council makes broad policy decisions about the operation of the church that various committees and individuals will carry out. *Example:* determining the worship times for the coming year.

3. *To give advice to another group.* An example is an educational advisory committee appointed to study a church's entire educational program and then report its findings and recommendations to the church council.

BUDGET. Is part of the overall budget for the church designated for the activities of your committee? If not, is there money available for your committee? If there is, what is the procedure for getting it? Must you make a formal request to the church treasurer for money? Or must you submit a budget request to the church council before your committee will have operating funds?

MEETING FACILITIES. Usually this is not a problem for church groups, but the moderator should know what meeting places are available at the church and what procedure he should follow to get them for his group. Does he contact the church office for the arrangements? What procedure does he use to get a key for an evening meeting? There's nothing more embarrassing than a committee gathering at the church and then learning that no one has remembered to get a key.

RELATIONSHIP TO OTHER COMMITTEES AND THE CHURCH COUNCIL. No church group can operate by itself, because the organizational workings of a church are closely interrelated. Let's say you are the newly appointed moderator of your church's youth education committee. To be effective, you must know what the other educational committees are doing, such as the adult education committee (if your church has one) and the youth committee. You must also be aware of the activities of the council and what affect their decisions will have on your operations.

What reporting procedure is expected from your group? Are the decisions of your committee written up and included in the newsletter that goes to the entire congregation? Are you expected to give an oral report of your committees' activities to the church council? Is a written report of your committee's work filed with the official church records?

TIME CONSTRAINTS. Both moderator and the members of a group must be aware of any time constraints before the group starts meeting. Is your group expected to accomplish a particular task by a particular time? For example, if you are appointed to the call committee for a new pastor, there is usually a deadline imposed on the committee. If the deadline is two months from the time the committee is appointed, both moderator and members must plan their meeting times to meet that deadline.

If your group is an advisory committee organized to study the problem of poor attendance at Sunday school, you need to know when a report is expected from your committee. Do you have three months, six months, or a year to study the problem? It's obvious that you must know the time constraints, if there are any, in planning the operations of any decision-making group.

HOW ARE THE MEMBERS SELECTED? Assume you've been recently appointed moderator of your church's stewardship committee. Do you appoint the members to your committee, or does someone else, say the council president? Or can members simply volunteer to serve on the committee?

If the group is a standing committee, what are the provisions for replacing the members of the committee? Do they serve for a given term? Or are their terms indefinite?

2. Determine the Specific Purpose for Meeting

Is it essential that the group get together? Are there decisions to be made that a group should make? If so what are the questions that need deciding?

Unfortunately, standing committees may meet whether they have any decisions to make or not. While these meetings can satisfy a social need for some of the members, a group shouldn't meet unless it must make some decisions.

It is the moderator's responsibility to determine if the group should meet. He should make that decision by consulting with other members of the group, however. There may be questions that need deciding that the moderator isn't aware of, which leads us to the next area—the need to plan the agenda.

3. Plan the Agenda

Some people argue that planning an agenda (the items to be discussed) for a meeting is a waste of time; the members know what they want to discuss and will bring up important questions at appropriate times in the meeting. Not so. To have effective meetings, the moderator must take time to build an agenda. An agenda:

1. Helps the moderator plan the meeting. He can arrange for resource people if necessary, plan for use of visual aids, and gather background information related to items to be discussed.

2. Offers members an opportunity to suggest what should be discussed at a meeting.

3. Guides the moderator in allocating approximate time to be used for each item to be discussed.

4. Makes committee meetings more productive by giving order and direction to the meetings.

5. Makes members aware of what will be discussed at the meeting so they can be prepared to participate.

6. Helps the moderator determine if an item is one

that the group should discuss, or one that can be decided in another way.

7. Helps protect the committee from the introduction of irrelevant contributions.

Agenda building is not an easy task. Often more agenda items are suggested than can be discussed at any one meeting. Decisions must be made about which items should be included. The moderator, when he builds the agenda, should get an indication from the members of his group about the importance of each agenda item—which items must be discussed at this meeting, which could wait until another meeting.

There must also be flexibility in agenda planning. There may be items to be discussed at a meeting that could not be foreseen. These, if they are crucial, will obviously take precedence over some of the less important planned agenda items. Discussion of a particular agenda item, though tentatively planned to take 15 minutes, may require an hour once the discussion starts. The planned agenda is a guide for a meeting, not a rigidly adhered to format. A moderator with experience, is able to sense when an agenda item is sufficiently discussed and a decision made. Too little discussion can lead to low quality decisions, and/or poorly accepted decisions. Too much discussion can waste time that could be profitably used for work on other problems requiring decisions.

How are agendas developed? What's the source of agenda items? The usual procedure is for the moderator to solicit agenda items from the members of the group. Of course the moderator, too, may have agenda items to add. One caution here, some groups depend on the moderator to offer all the items for discussion at the meetings. When this happens, the group may become quite mechanical, reacting only to items the moderator presents. In a sense the moderator then becomes the group, and the other members only legitimize his ideas. In other groups, if the moderator offers all the agenda items, the group members complain that his items aren't the important ones to be discussed, and the meeting becomes non-productive until some decision is made about agenda items.

To avoid these problems the moderator can solicit agenda items directly from the group. One way to do it is to send each member a form like the following, perhaps a week before the group meets.

REQUEST FOR AGENDA ITEMS

To: _____

Requested by: _____

Please return by_____to Horacio Grimley, Moderator, 1513 Togstad Drive, Madison, Wisconsin.

Please list agenda items you have for the next meeting of our committee. Indicate the approximate time you believe is necessary to discuss the item, and any necessary resources. (Slide projector, flip charts, etc.)

Agenda Item   *Approximate Time*   *Resources*
1.
2.
3.
4.

With this information the moderator can prepare the tentative agenda, listing the items on the agenda in some logical order. If there is time, the tentative agenda should be mailed to members of the group before the meeting.

At the meeting a first item of business is to discuss the tentative agenda and obtain concensus on the items to be included at that meeting, which ones might be held over, and which must be included but were not on the original agenda.

A similar procedure for agenda building should be used for each meeting of the group. In some instances the procedure will be much less formal. The moderator may simply call the members of the group, asking them for agenda items. Or the moderator may have sufficient items left over from one meeting to build an agenda for the succeeding meeting. The point is that agendas are considered before a meeting is held. Remember the example at the beginning of this chapter. The kinds of frustrations felt by the members of that church council are similar to the frustrations of any group that meets without knowing what it's supposed to do.

4. Prepare Introductory Remarks

The tone of a meeting and often its effectiveness depend on what the moderator says in his opening remarks. The cardinal rule is to be brief. The group members are not meeting to hear the moderator but to discuss the items they have submitted for the agenda. This doesn't exclude opening remarks, however.

A new group can learn much about both the moderator and the group itself from those first brief comments. They can learn something about how formal or informal the moderator will be. They also learn the purpose of the group, both the long-range purpose if it is a continuing group, and the immediate purpose. And they learn the specific purpose of this particular meeting; the agenda the members received prior to the meeting will have alerted them to the content to be discussed. During the opening remarks the moderator underlines that the purpose of the meeting is to make decisions about the agenda items—not only to share information. It's surprising the number of people that attend meetings and never understand the purpose.

The moderator also says what he expects of each member: (1) the importance of attending the meetings, (2) something of the activities he sees for the members, such as working in sub-groups, getting information, helping to carry out programs, and so on, depending on the overall purpose of the group.

The resources available to the group are explained—the amount of money, policy for inviting in outside resource people, meeting places, and so on.

The recorder for the group is introduced. This person should be appointed by the moderator before the first meeting (it can be a man as well as a woman). The moderator should tell the group when future meetings are planned, if that decision is known, and the times for the meetings. Finally, the moderator should present the tentative agenda to the group, getting approval for the items which have the highest priority.

It should take the moderator no longer than 5 or 10 minutes to get to a discussion of the tentative agenda. His purpose is not to impress the committee with his ability or his knowledge about the committee purposes. That will become evident as the meeting progresses.

5. Make Necessary Arrangements

Although it seems minor, the meeting room is important. It should be the right size for the group. A large room, with a small group meeting in the corner, can be cold and uninviting. A crowded stuffy room will negatively affect a group's activities. The meeting room should be well lighted, properly heated, and well ventilated. If possible, it helps for everyone in the group to sit around a table so every person can see every other person's face.

Depending on the size of the group, there are six alternative ways that tables may be arranged that will allow group members to see each other's faces, and yet provide a comfortable arrangement.[2] (See diagram on p. 31.)

Other arrangements to be checked include the availability of a chalkboard or flip chart, materials for name tags (if the members don't know one another), and extra copies of the agenda.

6. Decide on Methods and Equipment

We now know how to decide on what's going to be done at the meeting, and we know that the moderator

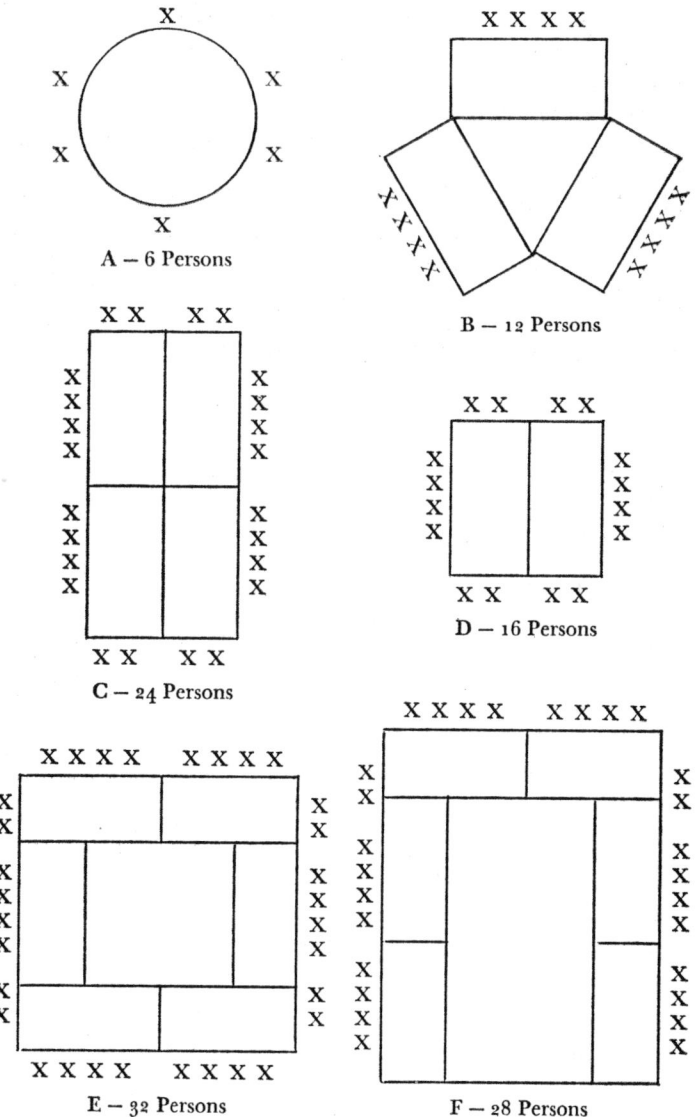

should make some introductory remarks to the total group. But what about the rest of the meeting? What should happen?

There are many ways to run a meeting, to keep it interesting to the members, and to make sure that the issues are thoroughly discussed so decisions can be made. Should visuals be used? Should the group be broken into small groups for some of the discussion? What are some approaches that assure that every member will participate in the discussion? These and other questions will be discussed in Chapter 8, "How to Involve Members" and Chapter 9, "Visuals Aid Understanding."

4

Decisions

In this chapter we'll look at some of the essentials necessary for decision making, in the next chapter we'll look at the decision-making process itself.

BACKGROUND FOR DECISION MAKING
Getting Acquainted

Before a group can effectively make decisions the members must know one another.

There are several techniques for getting people acquainted. Provide a name tag for each person. If the group sits around a table, fold 5 x 7 cards the long way, ask members to write their names on the cards with felt tip pens and place the cards in front of them.

At the first meeting of the group ask each member to share something about himself, his family, his work, and some of his interests. If the group is large, say more than ten, you could divide the larger group into smaller groups of two or three. Often a person is more willing to say something about himself to two other people than to a larger group. Once the members in the small groups are acquainted, each member can share a few things about himself with the total group.

Some group leaders feel introducing people is a waste of time. It would be better to get on with the task at hand. Yet, until a group of people knows something about one another, little productive work will take place.

And often the discussion about a particular problem will sidetrack while someone tries to learn something about someone else.

Developing Good Listening Habits

A second guideline is for group members to have good listening habits. What's the importance of listening to decision making? You're probably thinking: "I listen when someone else is talking," But do you? How often do you concentrate so hard on what you plan to say next that you hear little of what the person talking is saying?

If you're in a group where the members aren't listening, there's a simple technique to help correct the problem. Suggest, as a ground rule for part of a meeting, that before someone can speak he must summarize what the person speaking before him has said.

Now, before a person speaks, he must listen carefully. Some people are shocked at how poorly they do listen. Of course some people won't like the exercise. They'll resent having to repeat what someone else has just said, feeling it's a waste of time. It's often the person who is in a hurry to get things done who is the poorest listener.

A Group Matures

Groups need to mature. It takes time for a group of individuals who come together at a meeting, to become a dynamic, closely knit working group. Groups go through several stages before they reach maturity. I call these stages: *groping, griping, grasping,* and *grouping.*

When several people come together to work on a problem, they often wonder why they were selected, how long the job will take, what's involved in the problem—how complex is it, what problems are related to it, who else has worked on the problem before them, and so on. They are *groping.*

Most groups then go through a *griping* stage. A group

is in the griping stage when you hear comments like:

"This problem is impossible to solve. People have been working on this problem for years and couldn't solve it, what makes us think we can solve it?"

"We can't solve this problem with the budget we've got."

"The church council is thoroughly confused. Why don't they work on this problem themselves?"

They put the wrong people on this committee. We need experts not just ordinary people like us."

Nearly every group goes through a griping stage. For some the stage lasts only a few minutes, for others it may go on in one form or another for a year. Some groups fall apart during the griping stage. There is so much griping, the moderator and the group members believe all the gripes and they decide they can't complete the assignment they were given.

It's important to recognize that griping is a normal part of the maturing process. A group must work itself through this stage, recognizing that there will be gripes.

Grasping is the next stage. It occurs when there is a glimmer of hope, when people start understanding why they were brought together, when they start accepting others as peers and trust them, when some of the griping stops.

Most groups move quickly from the grasping stage to the *grouping* stage. Now the group is starting to mature. People are talking and listening; the group understands its task and has confidence they can carry it out. The maturing process doesn't stop. As the group meets and works together, it will continue to become more mature. There will be sliding backwards, too. When a group completes an assignment and then undertakes a new task, some of the maturing process may reoccur. There may be some groping, even some griping, but the group that once reached a degree of maturity will likely regain it quickly.

How long does it take for a group to mature? It may

occur at one meeting, in a period of two hours. Usually it takes more than one meeting of a group. For some groups it never happens. Many people are concerned when a group doesn't accomplish much of its task at its first meeting. The group may have come a long way toward helping members get acquainted with each other, and in working toward beginning stages of maturity. Time must be allotted for maturity to occur. Until it does, the group will have difficulty with many of its tasks.

Several factors already discussed in this chapter will help a group reach maturity more quickly. Group members must know and trust each other. They must be able to talk to each other, and they must understand what each other is saying. They must be able to listen.

The moderator and the group members must also have some understanding of the decision-making process. Failure to understand the decision-making process is a major reason why many groups never mature and thus never become productive groups.

NEED FOR DECISIONS

Within the church, and most other organizations too, there are three primary decision areas.

Reoccurring Decisions

These are the decisions that standing committees, church councils, and other groups that function in the church on a continuing basis face each year. Most of them are predictable. A church council, for example, knows that each year it must make a decision on the fall worship schedule, that each year it must present a budget to the congregation, that each year it must consider a salary adjustment for the professional staff. An adult education committee knows that it has to make decisions about adult education programs and how they are to be carried out. The youth education committee has decisions to make each year about how to organize the Sunday school activities.

These decisions can be planned for some time in advance because the group responsible for making the decisions knows well in advance of the need for deciding.

Unmet Needs and Unsolved Problems

These are not known in advance, but come up if programs are not functioning well, if a pastor leaves, if there is some sort of natural disaster like a fire, if there are complaints.

Some of these problem areas can be given to existing committees, for decision, but often a new committee needs to be appointed. These are the decision areas that usually cause the most strife in the church, and often take a good deal of time.

Opportunities

The need for opportunity decisions comes from comparing what the church is doing now with what it should be doing. Ideas for "what should be" are obtained from reading what other churches are doing, by talking with other church people, by constantly looking at the church in relation to the changing society, by the church looking critically at itself and asking if existing programs can be improved.

The opportunity decisions are often the easiest to overlook or not find time to consider. Often, if opportunity decisions are not considered, they become "unmet needs and unsolved problems." Unfortunately, many committees and other policy and planning groups in a church are so busy with routine reoccurring decisions and putting out the fires of complaints because of problems, that opportunity decisions come in last place priority. More attention to opportunity decisions could cut down on the time necessary for making decisions about program inadequacies based on complaints.

TYPES OF DECISIONS

Within most organizations, and especially within the church, there are four broad types of decisions: (1) planning decisions, (2) structuring decisions, (3) implementing decisions, and (4) recycling decisions.[1]

Planning Decisions

Planning decisions are usually made by policy groups such as the church council, and by various kinds of committees that have an advisory function. Planning decisions come by answering questions such as:

1. What are the top priorities of our church?

2. What are the top priorities of the various programs within the church, such as the education program, the women's organization, the worship activities, the older youth program?

3. Should the program goals of the church be changed? Should social action receive more attention than it's now getting? Where does adult education stand in relation to other church goals?

4. What problems does our church have in meeting the top priority needs?

Organizing Decisions

What are the means necessary to achieve the ends noted in the planning decisions? To make organizing decisions, variables like personnel, schedules, facilities, budget, and content must be considered. For example, a church council may decide that adult education will receive high priority for the next five years. Organizing decisions involve deciding how that goal can be implemented. Does the church need additional paid staff, a new recruitment program for volunteer adult leaders, additional budget for teaching resources, a revision of the present organization for worship to accommodate adult education activities?

Implementing Decisions

These are the decisions necessary to carry out the plan determined above. How will volunteer leaders for an adult education program be recruited and by whom? Exactly what will the adult education program be, what content will be included, what resources will be used and how, and so on.

Implementing decisions are those made by groups responsible for actually carrying out a program. The decisions are made within the framework of a plan.

Recycling Decisions

As a particular program operates, it is continually evaluated to see if its objectives are being met. If there are problems with any part of the program, then new decisions must be made—or old decisions must be reworked and reconsidered. For example, if a decision was made about Sunday worship that resulted in one service not being able to seat all the worshipers at that time, then the decision about the worship schedule will likely need to be reconsidered, and perhaps a new one made to solve this problem.

Recycling decisions are being made all the time, as programs in the church continue. The need for these kinds of decisions can be compared to a person driving a car. Little corrections are constantly made with the steering wheel. Recycling decisions are necessary to keep a program on the road planned for it.

Where are these various types of decisions made? As mentioned earlier, planning decisions are usually made by policy making groups. Organizing decisions, implementing decisions, and recycling decisions are made by the various program committees and organizations of the church, but these groups may also have responsibility for planning decisions. The women of the church, for example, may make decisions about the priorities for their program, determine a structure for carrying out the plan, actually carry out what was decided, and then constantly evaluate and make new decisions based on how things are going.

5

The Decision-Making Process

In the past 20 years considerable research has been done on how groups make decisions. Some of that research is summarized here in a way that should be useful to both group members and moderators, indeed for anyone who works with others to make decisions and solve problems.

We'll consider the following components of the decision-making process:
1. Clarifying the problem
2. Suggesting tentative solutions
3. Evaluating solutions
4. Agreeing on a solution
5. Taking action

The process of decision making, though it appears to be a step-by-step process, in reality doesn't work that way. Group members don't always clarify a problem and then smoothly and efficiently move through the various steps until they agree on some action. The group may move from clarifying the problem to evaluating solutions, and then move back again to clarifying the problem. Many groups work on evaluating solutions and then find they must go back and develop more tentative solutions. So the process of decision making is not as straight forward and simple as working through five steps. In practice the process is much more complex and dynamic.

CLARIFYING THE PROBLEM

One of the first places to start in clarifying any problem is to try and locate it. Is the problem located in an individual, in a situation, or in a group?

Let's say you are a member of your church's education committee, and your committee has received several complaints about the Sunday school program. Some of the comments have been: "Our kids hate to go to Sunday school this year; they'll do just about anything to avoid going" or "My child gets nothing out of Sunday school; it doesn't mean a thing to him."

Your committee also has learned that attendance since Sunday school started last fall has dropped by 50 percent, and several teachers have quit without offering any good reason why.

What is the location of the problem? Does it rest in *an individual,* say the Sunday school superintendent or maybe the pastor? Are those responsible for the preparation and inservice training of Sunday school teachers not doing their job?

Does the problem rest in *the situation?* Are there inadequate facilities? Perhaps the rooms are too crowded, or the noise levels are too high. Are the times scheduled for classes in conflict with parents' schedules? Are the curriculum materials satisfactory? Can both teachers and students work well with the materials?

Is the problem in *the group* involved? Do the Sunday school teachers have problems working with each other? Are their relationship problems between the Sunday school superintendent and the teachers, between the pastor and the Sunday school teachers?

Once the general problem is known, then the specifics can be sorted to find the various dimensions of the problem. Usually a problem is located in several places at the same time: part of the problem may be in an individual, part in the situation, and part in the group involved. Locating the specifics of the problem is then the first place to start in clarifying any problem.

Problems and Solutions

Occasionally problems are stated in such a way that they really are one form of a solution. This is often subconsciously done by members of a group, for there is the natural instinct to immediately move to ways of solving a problem without spending much time trying to clarify it.

For example, someone in the group dealing with the Sunday school complaints may say the problem is: "How can we get the Sunday school superintendent to hold more meetings?" He assumes the problem is located in the Sunday school teacher and how that person operates. That may be a totally inaccurate assumption, and the group that then spends time figuring out a way to get the Sunday school superintendent to hold more meetings may not be dealing with the real problem at all.

One Approach

Here is one approach a group can take to help clarify problems and give decision making some direction. Let's assume you've been appointed moderator of a special committee to study the contributions of members to the church's program, with an emphasis on time and talent contributions.

Having shared that broad purpose with your committee, you may hear comments like the following:

"Everybody's too busy."

"That's the paid staff's job."

"Hire somebody if there's something that needs to be done."

"People who volunteer are usually poorly trained to do the job."

"What we gotta do is figure out what needs to be done then ask people to do it. Don't wait for them to volunteer."

The comments you usually receive are a combination

of suggested solutions and various interpretations of the problem. But usually people don't want to spend much time talking about the problem. They want to discuss how to solve the problem, even if they don't fully understand what it is. But clarifying the problem is essential in the decision-making process.

The following is a modification of an approach for problem clarification developed by Andre Delbecq, a University of Wisconsin researcher.[1]

Delbecq's approach starts with the assumption that the moderator of any decision-making group feels strongly that problem clarification is an important beginning place for decision making.

In the introductory remarks when this group first meets, the moderator might say, for example, "Our purpose for meeting is to study the contributions members of this congregation make to the church's program and suggest ways we can improve the situation." Following the Delbecq approach, the moderator would suggest the following procedure to help clarify the problem. If the committee has seven to nine members, the entire group can work as one. If it is larger, say 15 to 20, it should be broken into two smaller groups.

The moderator points out that most problems have two dimensions to them: (1) an organizational dimension and (2) an emotional dimension. The organization dimension includes such things as budget problems, lack of resources, organizational structure, and so on. The emotional dimension is how people feel about the problem, the anxiety, fear, or embarrassment they might have.

1. Each person on the committee is asked to list the organizational dimensions he can think of that relate to the problem of people not contributing time to the church's program. Everyone does this for approximately 10 to 20 minutes, working individually and not consulting with others on the committee. People would likely list such things as: "Nobody knows where help is needed." "How do we determine which jobs to hire done and

which to ask for volunteers?" Who will organize and supervise volunteer help?"

2. On another sheet of paper, everyone, again working individually, lists the personal feelings they have about the problem. Examples they might list are: "I don't like to volunteer—would help if I'm asked though." "Present-day church shouldn't have to depend on volunteers." "That's why we have a budget—so we can hire people." "It's the paid professional's job to make sure there's enough help." "I give money, isn't that enough?"

3. Someone from the group is designated recorder, and he or she writes each of the organizational problems on a flip chart with a felt-tipped pen. A round-robin system is used, each person in turn offering one of the organizational problems from his list. After each item is written on the flip chart, the moderator asks if others have the identical or a similar item. The number is recorded behind the statement. At this time there is no attempt to modify items so they fit into several broad categories. If there is any feeling that two items are not similar, both should be listed on the flip chart. When all of the organizational problems are listed, the recorder tears off the sheet and tapes it to the wall.

4. The same procedure is followed with the feeling items.

5. Now the members are asked to discuss the two lists, to clarify, elaborate, defend, or even add to the lists something someone overlooked. Again, the group should not try to group the items into categories. Specific dimensions of the problem are often lost when a summarizing procedure is followed.

6. The group is allowed 20 minutes to a half-hour for discussion, perhaps longer if the lists are long. Each member is then asked to vote privately for the five items that are most crucial on each of the two lists. The votes are tallied and recorded.

7. If there are two groups, they now come together and the votes of each group are reported to the total group.

The group then discusses the vote. (If there is but one group the discussion starts immediately.) Do they agree that the items receiving the highest votes are indeed those which should get prime attention? Is the group comfortable they have gotten into the problem in sufficient depth? Did the group have enough information to make the decisions they did?

Presenting the Problem to the Group

If the group is not involved in finding the problem, what are some guidelines for *presenting a problem* to the group?

1. *State the problem in situation terms, not in people terms.*

When a problem is stated in terms of how people must change, defenses come up and emotions often get high. When stated in terms of how situations must change, there is less defensiveness and people often change anyway, as the situation changes.

2. *State the problem specifically, usually in the form of a question.*

Sometimes problems are stated in vague or general terms to avoid hurting anyone's feelings. Problem as stated: "Our financial status is sometimes questionable." Translation: "How can we improve our church's bookkeeping system?" The moderator avoids the specific question because he doesn't want to hurt the financial secretary's feelings.

Some problems include several sub-problems. *Problem:* What can we do to improve attendance on Sunday morning? *Sub-problems:* How can we get parents to attend church with their children rather than dropping them off at Sunday school and coming alone? How can we get the "four-times-a-year" people to attend more regularly? What can we do about the drop in attendance during the summer months?

3. *The statement of problem should be brief.*

Moderators often spend too much time introducing a problem before discussion is invited. The moderator may fear that no one will say anything once he finishes introducing the problem. So he keeps on talking. A pause after the problem is presented is important and appropriate. Give people a chance to talk. There's usually a little reluctance for the first person to speak. But give the person a chance. And don't fear a moment of silence. A pause puts pressure on everyone.

4. *The moderator shares essential information.*

Besides presenting the problem to the group, the moderator should describe the time constraints (how soon must the group have an answer to the problem) and any budget limitations (must your solution fit a certain budget amount?).

It's important that the leader supply the information without trying to interpret it.

There are dangers if the moderator supplies too many facts about the situation. People can only absorb so much at one time. The more important facts may get lost among the less important, and people in the group may get the impression that the moderator has a preconceived solution in mind.

An important guideline is for the moderator to supply the essential factual information at the outset; additional information can always be supplied the group. Of course, the moderator faces the problem of sorting out what is essential and what is not.

5. *The statement of problem should encourage freedom of thought.*

As mentioned previously, the moderator must avoid suggesting a solution when the problem is presented. Otherwise the group will start debating the pros and cons of the suggested solution without thinking much about the problem.

SUGGESTING TENTATIVE SOLUTIONS

The first step when discussing a problem is to determine the attitudes of the group. How do people feel about the problem to be discussed? Is it a problem that has emotional dimensions to it? Let's use as an example how can our church improve its educational program? In discussing that problem what can be done to help people release their feelings. Here are some ideas that Maier suggests:[2]

1. Give Assurance.

The Sunday school teachers in your group may be threatened. Some may feel that one or more solutions may cause them to lose their jobs as teachers. If it is realistic and honest, guarantee the Sunday school teachers that they'll have an opportunity to teach. Another way to give assurance is to suggest that not everyone has to accept the changes suggested. Let's say one of the suggestions is to eliminate the Sunday school in favor of religious education conducted by the parents in their homes. That alternative will have much more chance of being accepted if people know that they don't have to accept it, but may continue to send their children to the traditional Sunday school.

2. Encourage and Provide for the Expression of Feelings.

If someone expresses a total unhappiness with how things are going, by all means let him talk. And don't try to judge what he has said, if you are the leader of the group. Simply accept the feelings as they are presented. This does not mean that you, as the group leader, necessarily agrees with the idea; it simply means that you believe everyone's contributions are worthy of attention by the group.

3. Create an Atmosphere of Understanding.

The following guidelines help insure understanding:

a. Every person has the right to say what he thinks, without interruption, and without judgment when he has finished.
b. Occasionally the group leader should ask members if they understand, to create a questioning environment.
c. If a person makes an unusual comment or presents an unusual idea, he should be asked to say more about it. The group, in so far as possible, should understand every comment that's made.
d. Participants should be encouraged to gave examples when they present ideas. Being specific often helps to clarify a position for the listener.
e. Restating the person's ideas in different words is a useful way to test understanding of an idea.
f. All the members of the group should be involved in the discussion. Pauses in the discussion encourage those not participating to do so. Ask the quiet person directly, for his opinion if he hasn't commented. (See Chapter 8 for a discussion of various ways of involving people in group discussion.) The leader must be cautious though; sometimes the quiet person feels threatened if he is called on, and he may also not have anything to say and may feel embarrassed.

One problem many groups have is to suggest the obvious alternative solutions and then move toward comparing them, rather than pushing themselves to consider more alternative solutions.

With the example, how can we improve our church's Sunday school, the group will likely suggest: recruit more teachers, provide better teacher training, obtain better curricular materials, and perhaps promote Sunday school more with the parents.

Sometimes it's necessary for the group leader to ask questions like: (1) Can anyone think of another way to do it, perhaps an alternative that no church has ever tried? (2) Can we get any clues for our problem from what's happening in other places, maybe outside of the church? (3) How can we improve on any of the suggestions that you've already made?

Let's say the group decides to discuss the alternative that the parents should be more involved in Sunday school for their children. Someone might suggest that interested parents be encouraged to hold Sunday school in their homes, either with several families or alone. Someone else may say, "Why not have an open Sunday school, patterned after some public education programs. Let the parents and the children determine what will be taught, how it will be taught, and where it will be taught."

With a little more probing, most groups will get past the superficial stage of providing the obvious alternatives. They probably aren't good alternatives or they would have been tried before, or they were tried before and they failed.

Another way to push for more alternatives to a problem is to delay the finalizing of the list of alternatives until another meeting. People often will think of the less obvious alternatives for solving a problem when they are away from the meeting. This is a particularly good technique if time constraints allow the group to spend more than one meeting looking at alternative solutions.

There are several things the moderator can do to keep the process on the track:

1. Keep the discussion on the task at hand. So often a group will want to debate the merits of a particular alternative rather than going on to list additional alternatives.

2. Check for understanding. Make certain that the group understands the various alternatives offered.

3. Summarize the progress of the group occasionally, to ease the frustration of those who believe the group isn't doing anything, and to help everyone keep the meeting in focus.

EVALUATING SOLUTIONS

At this point the long list of possible alternatives may be written on a blackboard, and the group discusses their relative merits. Sometimes, it's obvious that two or three of ten alternatives are the most promising, and the group chooses to spend most of its time on the two or three. Other times, more alternatives seem plausible, and then more of the alternatives are discussed.

One way to implement this is to write two columns on the blackboard or a flip chart. One is headed advantages, one is headed disadvantages. Each alternative is evaluated and the appropriate comments noted under each of the headings.

In any list of alternatives there are pet solutions that people have tried in other situations or have seen tried in other situations. Because a solution has worked in another situation does not mean it will work in your situation. Each alternative solution must be evaluated as it relates to *your* problem situation. Indeed an important question to keep asking is: Does this solution relate to this situation?

A final question to ask, to what extent does a particular solution create a new problem?

AGREEING ON A SOLUTION

The process of selecting a solution depends on (1) the size of the group, (2) the variations of interest in the group, and (3) the number and quality of alternatives available.

The process of agreeing on a solution can be more systematic if a list of criteria are prepared that would characterize the ideal solution. The process of finally selecting a solution then is one of selecting the solution that comes closest to the ideal.

Some possible criteria that could be used are:
  The solution will not cost more than the budget available.

The solution will be accepted by most of the people.
The solution is a new way of dealing with the problem.
The solution is possible with the resources available (number of pastors, office staff, size of congregation, etc.)

Of course each decision-making group must determine the criteria that best fit their problem situation. Without taking time to develop criteria, the group will have a difficult time making a decision about which solution to select.

In some situations the group may choose not to decide on any of the alternatives, to not make a decision. A group looking at the worship schedule for the coming year may consider several alternatives. They may discuss the relative advantages and disadvantages of each alternative schedule offered and then decide that they'll stay with the schedule they had. By not making a decision they have really made a decision—to select the alternative they have followed in the past.

Let's say your church has a personnel problem with the office secretary. The personnel committee may discuss the problem and may suggest several alternatives for solving the problem, yet decide to select none of the alternatives. They are hoping, with a decision not to act, that time may solve the problem, or someone else may solve it for them.

Occasionally a group may want to test a decision before it's finalized. A worship committee may suggest a new communion procedure, but wants to try it a few times, with special groups, before it is introduced to the total congregation.

Occasionally the group cannot agree on an alternative. Then the moderator may ask the group what it wants done. Should the group decide on a majority opinion? Do they want to suggest someone else or another group make the decision? (Perhaps two alternatives are presented to the church council and the council then makes the final decision on an issue.) Or do they want to continue to work toward some type of compromise to the solution of the problem?

In most instances, consensus is usually preferred to majority vote on issues. But there may be times when there is no other way to resolve an issue. Before voting, however, the group should agree that allowing a majority vote on an issue is acceptable.

Parliamentary Procedure and Decision Making

Some moderators, group members too, feel they must follow parliamentary procedure whenever they meet. There are many problems when parliamentary procedure is followed in a group decision-making situation.

Most of us have grown up with some introduction to the parliamentary procedure format. We know something about how to call a meeting to order, how to make and second motions, how to vote on motions, and all the rest.

And most organizations, particularly at their business meetings, follow parliamentary procedure. Because many people have had some exposure to parliamentary procedure and know something of how to use it, they carry this knowledge to the small group charged with making decisions. This is a mistake.

In almost every decision-making group, parliamentary procedure hinders rather than helps solve problems. Here's why. The key element of parliamentary procedure is the motion. But when someone makes a motion during the process of group decision-making, he usually short-circuits the entire process. By making a motion, the person prevents other solutions from being introduced until that motion is discussed and voted on. Following parliamentary procedure prevents discussing whether the problem the group is working on is properly understood. When the motion is made, the discussion must be on that motion. Any other discussion is out of order if the rules for parliamentary procedure are followed. Here's an example:

Five members of an office staff are on a committee to plan the annual office picnic. The moderator of the committee ask, "Any ideas on the office picnic?"

John Sims, a member of the committee says, "I move we have the picnic at the city park again this year."

And Sally Sommers says, "I second the motion. We were there last year and that's a good place."

You can see what will happen. If the moderator is a strict parliamentarian, he will ask if there is any discussion and then the five people will vote on the motion. Why is this not a good procedure?

In the first place there was no discussion about the committee's problem. Were they supposed to plan the office picnic and stop with that? Or are they supposed to plan the picnic and then carry out the plans? Were the five of them to plan and organize the picnic by themselves or could they ask others to help with the work once the planning is done?

When John Sims made the motion, the entire committee was sidetracked into thinking about his suggestion, before they even had a chance to discuss the purpose of the committee.

And maybe some of the people on the committee aren't too sure they want to go to the city park again this year. Perhaps they'd like to offer additional suggestions for consideration. In fact, some of them may want to talk about an entirely different kind of office get together compared to last year's.

Parliamentary procedure and motion-making prevented all of that from happening. For most small decision-making groups, motion-making is best avoided.

When There Is Conflict

Often during a meeting there will be conflict. Conflict doesn't always have to be negative. But for conflict to be positive there must be conflict of ideas, not conflict of personalities. Conflict, to be productive, must focus on the ideas being presented and not on the individuals presenting the ideas. If the difference of opinion gets to the name-calling stage, then any positive outcomes are lost.

What are some of the positive outcomes of conflict of ideas? The quality of the decision may increase if those who advocate differing points of view are forced to support their positions with logical arguments and factual information. Often new ideas and new solutions come out of these discussions.

"When the solution to a problem involves the resolution of a conflict between individuals, attitudes and feelings become a crucial part of the problem situation. Solutions to such problems must fit their needs, and objective, factual considerations play a secondary role. The major goal is not that of finding a 'correct' solution, but rather one of finding a solution that achieves the highest acceptance." [3]

TAKING ACTION

What is the group's responsibility in putting the solution into effect? If the group making the decision has the responsibility for implementing the solution it just agreed upon, then it must decide what duties each person will assume, the steps involved in implementing the decision, the follow-up necessary to test the effectiveness of the decision, and whether additional meetings should be held to evaluate the results of the decision.[4]

If the group is an advisory group, the only action it might take is to communicate the group's decision to whoever has asked for the advice, perhaps the church council. The group should decide who will make the report, and the form that the report will take. Perhaps several people in the group will work with the moderator or the recorder in writing the final report.

If the report is to be an oral report to the entire congregation at the annual meeting, then both the content of the report and how it will be presented must be decided. Will visuals be used in the presentation? Will other members of the group be involved in presenting various parts of the report?

Deciding on what is to be done, who is to do it, how it is to be done, when it is to be done and where, are essential considerations for any decision-making group.

ALTERNATIVE APPROACHES

Some groups may not wish to follow the approach outlined above, but wish to follow what Brilhart calls the "Reflective-Thinking Sequence." [5] This process includes three phases:

1. Determining the nature of the problem
2. Suggesting and evaluating solutions to the problem
3. Putting the solution into effect

Another, slightly more elaborate Reflective-Thinking Sequence includes the following phases:

1. Define and limit the problem
2. Describe, analyze and evaluate the problem
3. Establish criteria by which solutions may be judged
4. Evaluate the probable consequences of each possible solution
5. Select the preferred final solution
6. Plan how to put the solution into effect.

These are but two of many different types of problem-solving approaches that may be followed. In an article in the *Journal of Creative Behavior,* McPherson describes 18 different problem solving approaches that have applications to a wide variety of situations: the military, industry, and business, for example.[6] Perhaps in your church, you'll want to modify the approaches suggested in this chapter to better fit your situation.

6

Understanding Group Members

When you work with groups, you'll find many different types of people represented. Because of differing experiences, personalities, educational levels, and a host of other reasons, each person is unique and behaves quite differently from any other person. Most of us would agree that this is good. No one wants to work in a group where everyone thinks and acts the same way. But when there are differing viewpoints represented, and when each person acts according to his beliefs, there can be difficulties when these people attempt to solve problems and make decisions.

Let's visit a church's nominating committee as they discuss nominations for church officers. The committee has been asked to select two candidates for the offices of president-elect, secretary, and council member. Let's assume in this church half of the officers and council members are elected each year. The problem for the committee then, is to select two candidates for each office. There are four people on the committee.

Fred Smith, vice-president of the local bank, is moderator. Fred, who is middle-aged, slightly overweight, and balding, is quite authoritarian. He wants to get things done as efficiently as possible.

Angie Davis is a homemaker, middle-aged and attractive. She's someone most people would say was easy to get along with.

Joe Thomas is a local high school teacher. He's young, out of college only two years, and very people-oriented. He believes in the dignity and importance of every person.

The fourth person on the committee is Florence Reed, an older woman who has many years of organizational experience. In recent years she has become impatient with committees and how they function, to the point where she questions whether a committee is the best way to get problems solved.

At the first meeting, the moderator Smith is speaking: "You all know why we're here. We're supposed to come up with names of two people for each of these three council positions that'll be open. What do you say we start with the president-elect. We've gotta come up with two good names; this person's going to be our congregation president in a couple of years. We've gotta give this decision some thought.

"I'll write the names on this sheet of paper as you give'm to me. All right let's go. Who do you suggest? I'm hoping we can get this meeting over in an hour or so."

Florence Reed sits staring out the window, obviously bored with the entire procedure. She pokes Angie Davis and says:

"Same old bunch of junk isn't it? Big waste of time. Here we sit fussing with names. Why can't the present officers just suggest two names for each office? Can't see why we should waste time with it."

She continues, but now is a low whisper: "You hear about the trouble Fred Smith is having with his wife? I heard the other day that she's gonna leave him. Can't say as I blame her. He's nothing but a stuffed shirt. Just look at him, all excited about our suggesting names for offices, you'd think that was all he had to worry about. He oughta be home talkin' to his wife."

Joe Thomas says: "Mr. Smith, I hate to sidetrack what you're asking, but I've only been in town a few months and I don't know these other two people. How about our introducing ourselves to each other?"

Smith answers: "Sure, go right ahead."

The four people introduce themselves to each other and there's some small talk about where people work and so on.

Smith: "Well, it's time we get going. We're already behind time. I wanted to wrap this all up in an hour. Looks like it'll take us a little longer than that. Let's get back to our task, who do you suggest for the president-elect?"

Angie Davis: "How about Jess Mitchell?"

Florence Reed: "Nah, not Jess, he hasn't done anything for the church since he joined, doesn't even come to worship services regularly. All he's got is a big mouth. What he says sounds good, but when it comes to work, well he's just plain lazy—like a lot of other people in this church I might add."

Smith: "Well, what about Jess Mitchell? Do we keep his name or not?"

Thomas: "I think we oughta write his name down. We can cross it off later. I really don't know much about Mitchell, but I think we should at least consider him for the time being."

Angie Davis: "You know, I'm a little confused. Why don't we spend some time talking about the type of person we think would make a good president? Maybe I shouldn't have offered Mitchell's name. Maybe we first should write down some of the qualities we think a president should have. What do you think?"

Florence Reed shrugs her shoulders, not really caring what the committee does. Joe Thomas shakes his head yes, and the moderator says: "I suppose we could do that all right, but it's gonna take a lot of time. I think we all know what kind of person we want for president-elect and if we're gonna get this job done we've gotta come up with more names. Anybody got another person in mind? I've got Mitchell's name written down."

TYPES OF GROUP MEMBERS

Let's leave the nominating committee and talk about the kinds of people in groups and what they do. Nearly every group has three kinds of people.

First, there are those who are most interested in getting something done. They're called *task-oriented*. Task-oriented people are mostly concerned that the assigned task be completed, that the problem the group has be solved.

Secondly, there are *people-oriented persons*. They are first concerned about the feelings of others and that groups provide an atmosphere where people can feel secure and comfortable. Those in this second group are called *group-maintenance* people. They're more concerned about keeping the group together and helping people better relate to one another.

So the two basic types of people in most groups are task-oriented people and maintenance-oriented people (people-oriented persons).

The third group of people found in most groups can be best described as *"all-for-me" people*. They aren't interested in what problem the group is trying to solve, nor are they interested in keeping the group together. They are attempting to meet some personal need. Their input to meetings is often negative.

Let's look at the meeting of the nominating committee again and determine what kinds of people are there. If you guessed that the moderator Fred Smith is a *task-oriented* person, you're right. His concern is for the group to work on its assigned task, to solve the problem in the most efficient way. He's often disturbed by suggestions that he perceives as slowing down the process or moving the group away from the problem at hand. Remember how he said at the very beginning of the meeting that the committee members all knew what the problem was and they should get right at it. He then asked for the names of people who might be candidates for president-elect. Later, when Angie Davis suggested the committee talk about what kind of president-elect they ought to have, Smith saw this as getting them away from their problem. He wanted the group to work on suggesting names and wasn't willing to listen to anything that would suggest a diversion from that task.

What kind of person is Angie? *Task-oriented* or *maintenance-oriented?* She too might be classed as a task-oriented person, but she acted differently from Smith. In one instance she was willing to go along with Smith's suggestion that they offer names. But another time she was concerned that he wasn't using good problem-solving procedure, and she suggested the group spend some time talking about what kind of president-elect they ought to have. Her concern was with task, but she was also concerned with how the group perceived the task or problem to be solved. She was questioning Smith's judgment that they suggest names for the offices without some guidelines.

How about Joe Thomas, the high school teacher? Obviously, Thomas is a *group-maintenance* person. He wanted everyone in the group to feel comfortable at the meeting. He also is the kind of person who probably knows that for good problem-solving to take place, there must be some trust developed. The first step toward group trust is for the committee members to know one another.

Then there's Florence Reed. No question about Florence—she's a problem on this committee. She sat staring out the window most of the time; and when Jess Mitchell's name was suggested as a possibility for president-elect, she was against it. To this point in the meeting, her contributions were negative.

Both task- and maintenance-oriented people are needed in a group solving a problem. A group with members who are all task-oriented may never get the problem solved because of the tensions that may develop between people. And likewise, a group that has all group-maintenance people will never solve any problems either. A group with all group-maintenance people will be a happy group, people will enjoy belonging to it; but without some task-oriented people around, nothing much will get done.

As for the "all-for-me" people, nearly every problem-solving group has at least one. There are no easy ways of dealing with them. Sometmes they can be given tasks which may help make them contributing members of the group. Sometimes "all-for-me" members are best ignored. What's important, though, is for each member of a problem-solving group to recognize that there may be problem members in their group.

Within each of the broad classifications of members: (1) task-oriented, 2) people-oriented, and (3) "all-for-me" members there are specific types of group members.

TASK-ORIENTED MEMBERS

"Let's Get Started"

Let's-get-started people are those who will say at the beginning of a meeting, "Well, what are we waiting for. Let's get going." Let's-get-started members are goal-oriented and can't see much need to spend time on preliminaries. Time spent introducing members and getting acquainted is considered a waste of time. These members feel that meetings are held to get something done and anything that detracts from working toward the overall goal is a waste.

"Where-to?"

Where-to? members are concerned with knowing exactly where the meeting is headed. They want to know what the outcome of the meeting is supposed to be. A *where-to?* member is not willing to spend time on group work unless he knows exactly what the group is supposed to do.

Question asker

The *question asker* helps clarify the issues. He asks questions that other group members are often reluctant to ask. You've likely attended meetings when someone has said, "And it seems that it's the prerogative of this committee to develop an integrated plan which will be endorsed and accepted by the power structure of this organization and which can be implemented with a minimum expenditure of participant time and energy."

After a mouthful like that there's often complete silence. The *question asker* isn't afraid to ask, "That sounds impressive, but what are you talking about?"

Answer giver

The *answer giver* is willing to share personal experiences and other information he has when it relates to the question discussed. He wants to see the group progress toward its goal and is willing to share what he knows to help.

Summarizer

The *summarizer* helps a group see the important elements that have been discussed, and what yet needs to be done. By doing this, the *summarizer* helps the group stay on the subject and focus on where it's been and where it's going.

All five of these roles are concerned with getting a job done and helping the group reach its goals. But there is more to group work than reaching goals. A group that's entirely goal-oriented, represented only by the kinds of people we've just described will have difficulties.

A committee can be compared to a musical group. Some in the group sing the melody. They, by their singing, give the listener the heart of the song. But for the musical group and the listener alike, a group made up only of those singing melody can be monotonous and uninteresting. So musical groups have people that sing harmony—people that add another dimension to the musical performance to make it more interesting and appealing to the listener and to the performer alike. The people who sing harmony in a group are the people-oriented members.

PEOPLE-ORIENTED MEMBERS
Supporting Members
The *supporting* member encourages contributions by other members. When someone offers an idea, he might say, "That's good, that adds to our discussion." By making that comment he's creating an atmosphere that will encourage others to feel a part of the group so they too will feel their comments will be favorably received.

Peacemaker
Picture two group members, Sam Olson and Tom Williams, arguing with one another. After a few exchanges back and forth these two men may start raising their voices. The *peacemaker* is the person who chimes in with, "Well, I guess we all know where Sam and Tom stand on this issue. Wonder who else has an opinion?" This comment from the peacemaker helps relieve the tension. And it provides an out for both Sam and Tom, who now have some time to "cool off" and think about what they've been saying. Another technique the *peacemaker* often uses is to identify some element in the argument to which both parties can agree. This can help bring the argument back to a discussion of the issue.

Controller
The *controller* helps throttle the person who wants to dominate a discussion. When one member talks on and on, and no one else has an opportunity to speak, the controller may say, "Let's hear from Joe Wilson. Anything you have to add to the discussion, Joe?" With that tactic, the controller has subtly shifted the conversation and hopefully squelched the over-talkative person, at least for the present.

These three types of group members help a group maintain a warm, friendly atmosphere.

Obviously both task- and people-oriented members are both needed for a group to operate effectively. Occasionally a group will have the balance between task- and people-oriented members disrupted. Too much people orientation and the group will likely not accomplish much. Too much task orientation and the group might fall apart. There must be a balance between the two in a meeting.

"ALL FOR ME" MEMBERS

Because "all for me" members usually act in a way that neither contributes to the group achieving its goal nor to keeping the group together, let's look at some ways for dealing with each of various types of "all for me" members as we describe them.

Bragger

This person is interested in getting recognition by boasting of his achievements and acquaintances. This is the kind of person who's apt to say, "In my letter to the national church office last week, I indicated . . ." Or, "When I studied at the university . . ." To handle the *bragger,* politely ignore him. The group members will likely ignore him too. This treatment may help the bragger become a useful committee member. Of course there are times when it won't work, because some people don't realize they are braggers.

Fighter

This person is opposed to every idea or comment presented. Nothing pleases him and he wants everyone in the group to know it. Remember Florence Reed from the nominating committee. Florence is a *fighter.*

What does a group leader do with a *fighter?* Try to use humor. And let the other group members react to any obvious misstatements that the fighter makes. Another solution is get this kind of person working on a group project. This may get him or her interested in the group and doing some things that can't constantly be opposed.

Show-Off

The *show-off* is easy to spot. This person writes on the table cloth, tells his neighbor some gossip he heard this morning, laughs louder than anyone else, and participates in a host of other disrupting activities. Ask the show-off a direct question; it may cause him to start thinking about the group's activities.

Talker

No matter what the question or issue the *talker* has an answer and usually a long one. He enjoys the sound of his voice, but the others soon tire of him. When the talker stops for a breath, thank him and move on, perhaps asking another person in the group to comment on the issue. The *controller* mentioned earlier may also help the group leader control a talker.

Turtle

The *turtle* is the opposite of the *talker*. He pulls his head into his shell and doesn't say a word during the entire meeting. With a little encouragement a group leader can get the turtle to talk. Compliment him the first time he says anything. Ask this quiet person a direct question you feel he could answer easily. Often the turtle has a great deal to contribute once he's encouraged to open up.

If a group has a high incidence of "all for me" members compared to task- and people-oriented members, there may be some problems in the group itself. This may call for the group to step back and look at itself.

"The diagnosis may reveal one of several of a number of conditions—low level of skill-training among members, including the group leader; the prevalence of authoritarian and laissez-faire points of view toward group functioning in the group; a low level of group maturity, discipline and morale; inappropriately chosen and inadequately defined group tasks, etc." [1]

Much of the success of a meeting depends on the moderator's ability to recognize and deal effectively with the different kinds of personalities represented by the group.

The first step for the moderator is to be able to recognize the different types. He must be able to determine which members are primarily interested in goals and which members are primarily interested in keeping the group together. "All for me" members are most easily recognized, as their contributions or lack of contributions often result in problems for the group leader and for the whole group.

Once the moderator is able to recognize the roles played by group members, he can lead the group in accomplishing its goals and insure individual well-being by balancing the contributions of the various members. Occasionally certain roles necessary for effective group operation won't be represented by the members of the group. If this occurs, the moderator must assume the missing roles. For example, a group may not have a summarizer. Then the moderator must assume this role.

Group members don't always play the same role at meetings, which makes the job of recognizing roles more difficult. Occasionally the same person, during the course of a meeting, will perform both task- and people-oriented roles. Generally, though, a member will tend to perform roles that are either task- or people-oriented.

Certain forces at work on group members can affect the roles they play at group meetings. For example, if a person has a sick child at home, his performance at the meeting may be affected. A member's employer may have said to him before the committee meeting: "Now here is where I stand on the issue you're discussing tonight, and I'm sure you'll want to express an opinion at the meeting that agrees with your place of employment." This member will likely respond differently had he not received this message from his boss.

The perceptive moderator is able to spot exceptions to the way people normally act at meetings. The moderator also knows there are patterns of roles that people play at meetings. Being aware of these patterns can help the moderator as he tries to blend and mix the various roles to achieve successful meetings.

7

The Group Leader

One of the keys to good decision making is the group leader or moderator. What the leader does and how it is done often determines if group meetings are successful or not.

CHARACTERISTICS OF AN EFFECTIVE MODERATOR

Though there may be some exceptions, the following characteristics are important for people who will assume leadership roles with groups.

Impartial

An effective moderator insists that both sides of a question are heard. He avoids granting privileges to some and not to others, whether deliberately or accidentally, He learns to know when he is favoring one point of view and tries to avoid repeating this behavior. The leader in many instances has his own point of view on an issue, yet he must not allow his position to dominate the thinking of the group.

Able to Communicate

An effective moderator must be able to express ideas clearly to a group. Everyone in the group must understand what he is saying when he presents a problem (when it is necessary for him to do that) and when he is presenting factual information. Often the moderator must represent the group with other groups; occasionally he may have to speak to the entire congregation about the activities of his group. (See Chapter 11 for some tips on being a better speaker.)

Gets Along Well with Others

An effective moderator relates well to members of the group, so they will enjoy working with the leader, and also with one another.

Willing to Remain in Background

An effective moderator has confidence in the skills and abilities of the members of the group. Groups accomplish more when the moderator keeps attention focused on the issues and on other members of the group. The leader who constantly tries to impress group members with his vast knowledge and ability soon loses effectiveness. The role of the moderator is to guide the progress of the group and assure that contributions of all members are expressed.

Even Temperament

An effective moderator is not easily annoyed. Some members pride themselves on "getting to" the group leader. Once a group leader demonstrates through words or actions that a member will anger him, his effectiveness drops quickly.

Patience

Group decision-making is democracy in action. But democracy is often a slow process. It takes time for various points of view to be heard. It takes time for people with varying backgrounds to think through the answer to a problem. Even though the process may be time-consuming, there are ways for the moderator who knows the decision-making process to speed things up and make decision-making meetings both efficient and effective—and at the same time insure quality decisions and member involvement.

Flexibility

An effective moderator is always prepared to change plans. No matter how carefully a meeting is planned, something may happen to force a change in plans. Although one approach may have worked previously, an effective moderator is willing to try something different. He's willing to listen to suggestions from the group for doing things differently, yet he must clearly have in mind what the group is trying to accomplish.

Has Group Leadership Skills

An effective moderator knows the decision-making process and he knows how to work with people to achieve the group's purposes. Though the moderator may have the characteristics listed above, he may fail if he lacks the skills necessary for helping the group reach its goals.

MODERATOR ROLES

What does the moderator do as he works with a group? What group leadership skills must he possess?

1. *Establishes and maintains a social climate.*

A moderator is responsible for helping a group get acquainted. He knows the importance of both group maintenance and group task roles, and he helps to insure that both of these roles are played in the group, either by members or by the moderator himself.

An effective moderator knows how to involve members in the discussion, drawing out the quiet person and preventing the talkative members from monopolizing.

He also knows the importance of conflict in group decision making, and he knows how to deal with it so it can make a positive contribution to the discussion.

2. *Guides the decision-making process.*

The effective moderator states the problem to be solved, or helps the group define problems.

Occasionally he summarizes the progress of the group, helping the group to see where they have been and what still must be accomplished.

The effective moderator insists on quality. He raises questions to make certain the problem is adequately clarified, that sufficient alternative solutions are presented—not only the easily identified solution alternatives.

The moderator helps the group evaluate suggested solutions in light of criteria the group has agreed on for a solution to be acceptable.

And lastly, the moderator makes certain that action is taken, that the group doesn't make decisions without also considering what will happen to the decisions once they are made.

What Determines the Role a Leader Will Play?

Fiedler says "The effectiveness of a group is contingent upon the appropriateness of the leader's style to the specific situation in which he operates." [1]

Fiedler points out three aspects of group situations that influence the leader's role:

1. *Leader-member relations:* how well is the leader personally attractive to the group members and respected by them?

2. *Task structure:* is the task to be accomplished determined by another group and passed to the decision-making group? For example, a group may be asked to determine the program for a banquet to honor a church's 50th anniversary. The decision has already been made that there will be a banquet and that there will be some kind of program.

3. *Position power:* what authority has the leader that is defined by the church's constitution and by-laws, for example. A church council president has position power by virtue of his elected position.

What does all of this mean? When the leader has little power or when the group hasn't developed a personal relationship with the leader, he is better off taking charge of the task to be accomplished than trying to first develop a better interpersonal relationship with the group. "Unless the leader takes charge of the task under these unfavorable conditions, his group is likely to fall apart." [2]

If the task to be accomplished by the group is highly unstructured, such as deciding what an adult education program in the church should be for the coming year, the leader should be highly considerate of the group members' feelings and opinions. For the group to be creative, the leader must be more permissive and nonthreatening to the group members.

However if the task is straight-forward, most groups expect the leader to give clear directions and orders. "The leader who under these conditions acts in a passive, nondirective manner will tend to lose the esteem of his group." [3]

Fiedler, as a result of this research with many groups summarizes this way: "Other things being equal . . . a group will be influenced more easily by a person who is liked and trusted than by someone who is hated and rejected." [4]

FOUR TYPES OF LEADERS

There are four types of leaders often found in group leadership situations—indeed in most types of situations where leadership is necessary.[5] Following are the advantages and disadvantages of each of these types.

Charismatic Leader

This is a person who tends to inspire a group by the kind of person he or she is. There are certain people that others tend to look up to and respect. Eisenhower and Winston Churchill were examples of this kind of leader.

The charismatic leader can be a problem when he is leader of a small group responsible for decision making. This type of leader usually doesn't see his role in relation to the total goals of the group. As a result, the charismatic leader often has a single approach for dealing with all problems. Catch words and phrases are used which stir up a group and sometimes get members excited about something that's not possible for them to do.

If the charismatic leader works at relating his leadership style to the group objectives, he can be quite effective. This kind of leader can help a group become a group by stimulating people to work together. The charismatic leader also provides a certain excitement to meetings, making group work an interesting experience. Again the caution—the excitement is positive as long as the group is working toward its goals, not simply awed by the charismatic leader.

Organizational Leader

The organizational leader is one who is interested in the technical processes of organizational activities. This type of leader often measures the success of groups in terms of speed and quantity of work accomplished. The organizational leader also may have certain "canned" approaches he uses, which can cause him to lose sight of a meeting's purpose.

The organizational leader puts extreme emphasis on getting things done, with too little emphasis on discussion and thinking. He expects people to follow his "foolproof" approaches for action. When this type of leader is in charge, the meetings can be boring with little commitment to the group's goals by the members. The leader often ends up doing most of the work.

An organizational leader can improve the planning and operation of meetings, however. He can make meetings more efficient, but efficiency must be balanced with group interaction and quality decision making.

Intellectual or Expert Leader

Some of the contributions this type of leader can make include:

1. Providing perspective, able to see the long-range goals in relationship to the short-range goals of the group.
2. Determining the relationships of various aspects of a problem.
3. Presenting problems to the group and skillfully summarizing discussion.

Some of the shortcomings of the intellectual or expert leader include an inadequacy to carry out the "action" phase of decision making, and often a lack of rapport with the members of the group.

"The intellectual leader can contribute to the participation of the group only by combining his overall perspective with the specific feelings of the group members." [6]

Informal Leader

The strength of the informal leader is his ability to be aware of people's feelings and his ability to work with people in a flexible, human way. One shortcoming of the informal leader is an inability to see beyond the immediate concrete situation, to see the problem at hand in relation to broader questions and issues.

But nevertheless the informal leader is one that can make many contributions to church meetings. To allow for the informal leaders and appreciate their value, the conception of what a leader is should be redefined in terms of the following basic tenets:

> (1) leaders are regular people, not one-man dynamos who know all the answers and do all the work; (2) leadership is developed, people aren't born with a mysterious leadership ability; (3) people who like to work with and are sensitive to other people are the best potential leaders; and (4) good leaders don't need to keep up a front of always being poised, independent, and decisive.[7]

The primary role of the informal leader is his ability to communicate feelings of group members to other leaders. Often informal leaders can predict how an idea will "go over" with other members of a group.

Any small-group leader may be a combination of two or more of the above leadership types. And within the decision-making group there may be represented more than one type of leader. Though someone may be designated chairman of the group, there may be other leaders. Indeed there are often one or more informal leaders in every group, no matter what type of leader the designated group leader happens to be.

8

How to Involve Members in Meetings

One way to make meetings more exciting for the participants is to involve them, give them an opportunity to do something, give them an opportunity to talk and discuss issues. People can be talked to only so long; most welcome an opportunity to talk back, to react to what was said.

Some approaches for involving people in meetings are:
1. Group discussion
2. Buzz groups
3. Individual involvement
4. Symposium
5. Illustrated presentation
6. Brain storming
7. Reality Games
8. Role Playing

1. Group Discussion

This is the technique most often used by decision-making groups with 10-12 persons or less. If the group is larger, it may be difficult to get participation from everyone. Handled properly by the moderator, group discussion allows the maximum participation by all members. Problems with the technique are group members who dominate the discussion and those who do not participate at all.

The moderator using group discussion can help maintain interest and keep the discussion moving by being aware of the various roles participants are playing, and assuming those roles that no one else is assuming. As we said in Chapter 6, there are group-task and group-maintenance roles which must be performed if a group is to be successful.

The moderator should also be adept at using the questioning approach to keep discussion interesting and to involve members. There are several guidelines to follow:

1. Use questions that begin with *how?* *why?* and *which?*

2. Ask some questions of the group as a whole and expect someone to volunteer an answer. If you get no response, then ask someone directly.

3. Be sure to ask the question before you call on someone for an answer. The suspense of not knowing who will be asked forces the entire group to think about the question.

4. Avoid asking questions that suggest their own answers: "We shouldn't have to spend much time on this proposal, should we, Tom?"

5. Don't be alarmed if the answer to a question comes slowly. Silence often means good thinking. Sometimes a half-minute or more of silence is the most useful thing that can happen to a group. The moderator should avoid trying to always fill "silent" periods.

6. Many questions asked by group members of the moderator can be turned back to the group. This technique often stimulates further discussion.

2. Buzz Group

When the group is larger than 10 or 12, you may want to break into groups of three or four to get more involvement. These smaller groups are commonly called buzz groups. With this technique, many people can participate at the same time, and they are more apt to participate when the group is small.

Here's how this technique might be used. Let's say you're moderator of your church's adult education committee, which has 15 members. The committee is responsible for planning and conducting the adult education activities in your church, which include classes on Sunday morning, mid-week evening classes, and providing assistance to the church organizations such as the couple's club, the women of the church, and the men's organization.

In planning these activities, you may divide the total committee into three groups of five each, one to discuss the Sunday morning class, one the mid-week program, and one the contributions to church organizations. After the small groups have worked together for a half hour (the amount of time will depend on the assignment), the entire group meets together again to hear and interact with each other about what was done in each subgroup.

Not only has the technique allowed everyone to participate more fully in the discussion, but the adult education committee has accomplished more in the same time by splitting the larger committee into three smaller buzz groups.

This technique also works well when someone makes a presentation on an issue and there is time for questions by the group members. For example, a building committee of 15 members has invited an architect to talk to them about his plans for a new addition to their church. After the presentation, the committee might be broken into three or four groups and each group asked to develop two or three questions that they would like to ask the architect.

When using this technique, the moderator must make certain that each buzz group knows exactly what it's supposed to do and how much time it has to do it. Each buzz group should designate a recorder-spokesman who will report the buzz group's discussion to the larger group. A meeting room with moveable chairs is essential when using this discussion technique.

3. Individual Involvement

One way to get individual involvement is to have group members work on particular assignments by themselves. They might, as we explained earlier, work by themselves to identify dimensions of the problem they are to work on.

Another kind of individual involvement Bergevin, Morris and Smith call the "Quiet Meeting." [1] This technique may be used as a part of a regular meeting, or it may, in some instances be the entire meeting.

"This technique is characterized by periods of silence and by occasional spontaneous verbal contributions by a member of the group. The periods of silence include meditation, concentration, and study about the topic which has been placed before them on a blackboard or easel. Freedom of expression is strongly encouraged." [2]

To be successful, this technique should only be used with a group of people who know one another well, and not at one of the early meetings of a group. Some of the things the quiet meeting can accomplish are: (1) clarification of thinking by the group members, (2) opportunity for people to relate their thinking to what has been discussed, (3) development of creative ideas, (4) opportunity for a group that has become bogged down to get started again, (5) opportunity for individuals to reflect on the previous discussion before they are faced with making a final decision on a question.

The advantages and limitations of this technique are:

1. ADVANTAGES
    a. This technique can help us to learn to make creative use of silence and to place a premium on thinking;
    b. A person can voluntarily express his needs in an uninhibited but thoughtful way;
    c. A sense of fellowship can result from the silence and meditation;
    d. A relatively deep level of thought can be reached.

2. LIMITATIONS
   a. Not all groups have members with enough self-discipline to get along well without guidance by a leader;
   b. Some people find it impossible to bear silence;
   c. The required physical setting is not always available (a place that lends itself to reflection and meditation);
   d. This technique requires that the participants have previously become acquainted.[3]

The quiet meeting could be profitably used in groups planning church programs, such as new worship formats or new educational offerings. After the group has discussed many alternatives, the moderator might suggest there be 15 minutes for thinking and meditation, to allow each member to sort out his thoughts.

4. Symposium

In a symposium several group members present material to the entire group. Assume you are moderator of your church's community assistance committee. Your committee is considering three projects for the coming year—providing Christmas baskets for needy families in your community, buying several new books for the hospital, and organizing a golden-ager's club open to all senior citizens in the neighborhood.

An efficient and interesting way to present information about each project is to ask committee members to present information about each of the proposed projects. Ask each committee member to present a description of his proposal in about five minutes.

With a large group, 15 or 20 members, you may ask the symposium members to sit in the front of the room. This isn't necessary with a smaller group; the respondents can speak from where they're seated.

Following the symposium presentation, the entire group may discuss what's been presented, or the group may be divided into buzz groups to raise questions they'd like to ask of the symposium participants.

When the symposium is used, each participant must know before the meeting that he'll be participating. One disadvantage of this technique is that not as much material may be covered as if one speaker discussed the different points of view. But the variety and interest created by having several people present different viewpoints outweighs the disadvantage of time efficiency.

5. Illustrated Presentation

There are times when the moderator will need to present information to the group: when he's introducing a problem, when he's orienting a group to its purpose, etc. The illustrated presentation is a technique to make such talks more interesting and more effective. What is involved is putting together good visuals with proper organization for a talk. (See Chapter 9 for a discussion of visual aids, and Chapter 11 for a discussion of speech preparation.)

6. Brainstorming

Brainstorming is a technique that may be used to obtain a large number of ideas about a problem, ideas that are then evaluated and used in the decision-making process.

If your group has less than 20 members, you may brainstorm with the entire group. If your group is larger than 20 members, you may want to break into smaller groups.

Assign a problem, set a time limit, and state the rules:
1. Criticism of ideas offered is forbidden.
2. Creativity is welcomed.
3. Competition is encouraged.
4. Quantity is desired.
5. Problem is kept in mind.

Give the group a time limit of about five minutes and

turn them loose. Make sure a recorder writes down all of the items mentioned. If you're working with a small committee, the brainstorm contributions can be written on a blackboard or a chart pad as they are offered.

Often this technique will jar loose a group that is bogged down. Most group members will find the experience quite satisfying, and most will be impressed with the quantity and quality of the ideas that come from the exercise. Using this technique may help the group that has trouble becoming a functional committee; after the experience, there is often more feeling of oneness.

There are some pitfalls in using the brainstorming technique. It cannot be used in a decision-making process. Don't use it as the last activity before a meeting is adjourned. The group members will probably go home very frustrated as to what they have accomplished and where the group is going in its deliberations. The brainstorming technique must be followed by planning and evaluation.

7. Reality Games

The technique of reality games grows out of Eric Berne's work made popular in the book *The Games People Play*,[4] but most of the games that Mr. Berne describes are in some way destructive to the participants.

Reality games are an attempt to take advantage of the theory of gaming, but for positive results. The difference between the games Berne describes and reality games is that in reality games the participants all know the rules. The roles and the objectives of the game are clearly defined.

There are several skills that can be perfected by playing reality games:

1. Exploring our own thought process and feelings in greater depth.
2. Being more sensitive, perceptive, and empathic.
3. Reflecting another person's thoughts and feelings.

4. Drawing out another person, and helping him clarify his thoughts and feelings.
5. Clarifying values.
6. Helping others clarify their values.
7. Integrating feelings, knowledge, and skill.
8. Confronting and resolving conflicts in order to strengthen and deepen rather than weaken relationships.
9. Creating a cohesive, supportive group which is capable of working together to accomplish both common and individual objectives.

To meet these objectives, games must contain the following elements:
1. A set of rules.
2. A clear statement of objectives.
3. The agreement of all the players to abide by the rules and objectives.
4. A procedure for critiquing or looking back at the process of each game.

The following game is one that may be used when a group is discussing issues where there is known division of opinion in the group. This game is also useful when there is potential for emotions to get high.

THE POSITION STATEMENT GAME

There's confusion, distrust, suspicion, misunderstanding, time wasting and boredom caused by people talking around an issue, avoiding it, implying but never saying clearly and simply what they feel, what they think, what they want, and how they see things.

Objectives
1. To state your position clearly, directly, and completely so that:
   a. You will know yourself better, and others will know you better.
   b. It will be harder for others to manipulate you, and you will manipulate others less.

c. Your relationships will be more honest and clear, hence more secure, and more stable.
d. Less of your life will deal with conflict and confusion.

Definition of positive statement

A position statement should make clear that you are talking about your position, and not some absolute truth. This can be done by starting with one of the following phrases: "My position is . . ." "From my point of view . . ." or "The way I see it . . ."

The position should include your feelings and your thinking on the issue. The complete statement of feelings includes:
1. Emotions such as hope, fear, love, hate, frustration, anger.
2. Needs and related wishes, objectives, or plans.

The complete statement of your thinking should include:
1. The here-and-now thoughts about the problem, the facts, how they relate to each other, how they relate to a wider whole, etc.
2. The point of view, which includes your assumptions, past experiences, prejudices, and beliefs you use in interpreting the problem.

Procedure

1. Divide into groups of three to five.
2. Think about the topic for five or ten minutes, jotting down notes regarding your position if so desired.
3. Try to include both your feelings and thinking about the issue.
4. Each person takes a turn stating his position. The other members of the group determine whether the statement compares with the elements of a position statement listed above.
5. Each person discusses how he felt in thinking through his position, and whether the process was useful and helpful or not; any difficulties in arriving at a position or in stating a position should be mentioned at this time.

Following a reality game, the group can discuss the issues using such techniques as the group discussion or the buzz group. If the reality gaming was successful, the group should be able to discuss the issues more easily now that the participants have had an opportunity to develop their positions on the question. See the book *Reality Games* for further game ideas.[5]

8. Role Playing

Role playing is an acting out of a situation or a particular circumstance, usually done with little preparation. It's a technique that is most useful to help a group understand various relationships among people.

Sometimes just describing a situation doesn't allow a decision-making group to really understand the problem. Acting out the situation can provide the extra impact necessary for more complete understanding.

Let's say the church council is meeting to make long-range plans for the church. One way to use role playing is to have the pastor play the role of the council president, the council president play the role of the pastor, a parent of a Sunday school youngster play the role of the Sunday school teacher, and a Sunday school teacher play the role of a parent. Each would act out the situation from the viewpoint of the person whose role they are playing, giving their views on what they think the church should be doing in the future.

Following a few minutes of role playing, the council then could go back to a group discussion and talk about what they learned during the role-playing sessions. During the role playing, opinions and feelings are often exposed that seldom are expressed during discussion.

In role playing, follow this procedure:

1. Select a problem situation. It must be as specific as possible.

2. Describe the characters. If the role playing situation is a complaint about inter-office communication in the

church office, the characters might be the secretary, the pastor, and the part-time staff assistant.

3. Select the players. Usually a person does not play himself.

4. Give each player a large card with his role lettered on it so the players can easily remember who is playing which role.

5. Allow the players a few minutes, five or so, to prepare.

6. Give the setting to the entire group and introduce the players.

7. Continue the role playing only until each player has responded enough to make his or her position clear.

8. Follow the role playing with discussion (a) by the audience as to why players acted as they did, (b) by the players as to how they felt as compared to how they acted, (c) of what was learned from the role playing.

Role playing is best suited:

1. To develop understanding of the feelings of people.
2. To develop understanding of the forces in a situation that block good human relations.
3. To get the other fellow's point of view and situation.
4. To understand human behavior.
5. When discussion doesn't get deeply enough into an issue or situation.

Some limitations of role playing include:

1. This technique cannot be used to accomplish highly complex objectives; it must be restricted to simple, clear-cut problems and situations;
2. There is often the temptation to use role-playing as a gimmick rather than as a means to encourage and facilitate learning;
3. The technique requires alert, careful direction; it is not an easy one to use effectively;
4. The role-play must be supplemented by the effective use of other techniques;

5. The group may become so involved in the technique that they neglect subject matter or content;
6. Role-players may become so involved in their roles that they manifest emotions of deep personal significance;
7. The prospects of playing a role can cause fear and anxiety in the players;
8. Some groups may reject this . . . technique.[6]

Involving a Resource Person

A resource person often can help a group reach a decision about a problem it's trying to solve. Before inviting a resource person the group must decide if it can get information in a better way. A resource person is only one source of assistance.

If a group plans to ask a resource person to attend one of its meetings, the group should be able to answer the question: Why do we need a resource person? Two situations where resource people can be helpful are:

1. When a group needs factual information that isn't readily available or factual material that the group must have interpreted before it is meaningful.
2. When a group seeks the experience of someone who has worked through a problem similar to one faced by the group.

For example, as moderator of your church's building committee that has responsibility for developing a recommendation for a church addition, you may invite an architect to present facts and figures on a proposed addition. The architect can interpret building information that may be readily available, but information that requires professional interpretation before it can be useful to your committee.

In addition, your building committee may invite a person who has served on a building committee from another church to share his experiences in developing a plan for an addition.

When considering a resource person, make certain the group doesn't place too much emphasis on what the resource person can do. Some groups feel they can turn over their responsibility for decision making to the resource person. Decision-making groups must realize that the resource person is only a source of information, that the group still has the responsibility of deciding what to do with the information.

A resource person can be only as helpful as the group makes him. The resource person is of most assistance when the group knows exactly what it wants from the resource person and the resource person knows exactly what's expected of him before he comes to the meeting.

9

Visuals Aid Understanding

Research reveals that we learn:
- 1% through taste
- 1½% through touch
- 3½% through smell
- 11% through hearing
- 83% through sight.

We retain:
- 10% of what we read
- 20% of what we hear
- 30% of what we see
- 50% of what we see and hear.[1]

If we take into account this research, we should strive to provide information by combining sight and hearing. Too often we rely only on hearing to communicate our thoughts, not recognizing how much more effective we could be if we used a visual aid to accompany the spoken word.

Some Principles for Visuals

When using visuals to accompany presentations at meetings, the following should be considered:

1. *The visual is necessary.* It helps to accomplish a specific purpose the user has in mind. Visuals are not used as attention-getting gimmicks.

2. *Visuals are built around ideas.* The visual should be seen as another way to communicate an idea.

3. *The visual must be easily understood.* No matter what type of visual is used, the audience must be able to quickly grasp its message.

4. *The visual must be accurate.* A misspelled word will detract and destroy much of a visual's impact. Facts and figures used in visuals must be double-checked for accuracy.

5. *The visual must be appealing.* If there's lettering, it must be clearly legible and neatly done. When using charts or transparencies, use but one point or comparison per visual. Consider as a maximum 6 to 7 words per line and a maximum of 6 to 7 lines per visual.

6. *People must be able to see the visual.* This principle is often violated. Someone brings a page from a magazine to a meeting, holds it up and only those seated next to the person can see it. Or someone writes on the chalkboard in the handwriting size he uses on paper, and it is not visible six feet from the chalkboard.

7. *The visual must be easy to operate.* The visuals you use should not be so complex that they detract from the message you are trying to convey.

Chalkboard

Every classroom in the country has a chalkboard, as well as nearly every other room used for meetings. Though the chalkboard reminds us of school days, it is still one of the most easily used visuals.

Some of its advantages are that it is (1) easy to use—all that's needed is a chalk and an eraser; (2) spontaneous—when someone wants to use it to illustrate a point, to summarize a discussion, or to record various group contributions, it's there for immediate use; and (3) it's inexpensive.

It does take some skill to use the chalkboard effectively. The user must learn to write large enough so the entire group can see, and if the person using the chalkboard is talking while he is writing, he must learn to write and not have his back to the audience.

Flip Chart

The flip chart, which is a pad of large sheets of paper on an easel, can serve essentially the same purpose as the chalkboard. If there is no chalkboard in a meeting room, a flip chart can serve as a good substitute.

It also has some advantages over the chalkboard. The sheets on the flip chart can be flipped back and forth during a discussion. They can also be torn off the pad and taped to the wall.

Broad-line marker pens work best on the flip chart, allowing everyone at the meeting to see what's written.

The flip chart can also be used like a regular chart; the material can be prepared before the meeting and then the sheets can be flipped over during the presentation.

The sheets can also be preserved if necessary, to be used at another meeting, or as a source of notes for the meeting recorder.

Charts and Graphs

Charts can be prepared for a meeting to list key points you want to make in a presentation—perhaps in your opening comments to a committee, or in a summary of a problem you are presenting to a group. Charts are easily made and they can be reused many times. Other than an easel to support them, charts require no special equipment.

A graph, a special kind of chart, is a good choice when you want to show numerical relationships such as presenting budget material at a congregational meeting. Following are two examples to show how a graph may be used:

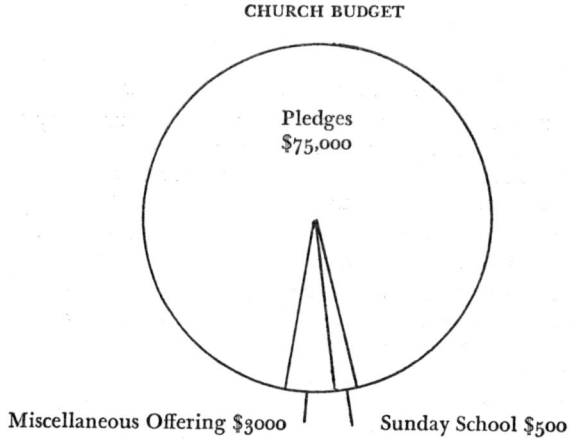

Income

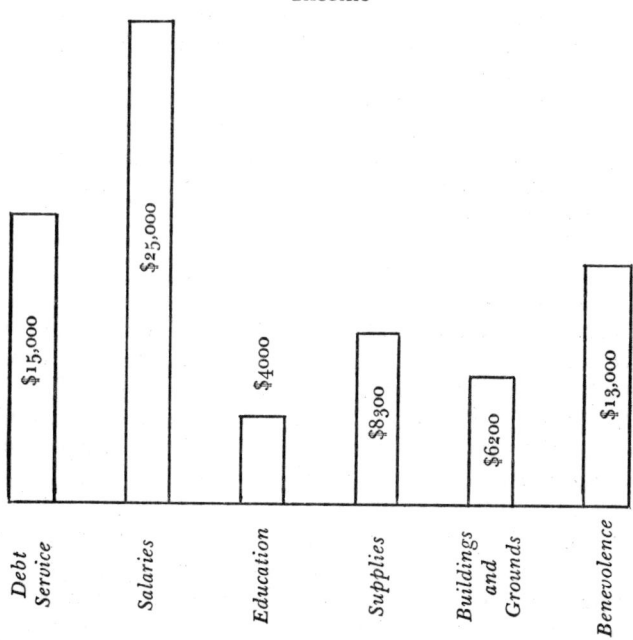

Expenses

Auger lists the following suggestions for using charts and graphs:
1. Cover the charts until they are ready for use.
2. Stand to one side of the chart with your body turned as much as possible to the audience. Turn your head, but not your body, as you refer to items on the chart. Use a pointer.
3. Tell the story of each chart fully and quickly and then return to each item for emphasis and review.
4. Don't expose the next chart until you are actually ready to talk about it. Otherwise, your audience will be diverted and will not hear what you have to say.
5. Lead from one chart into the next with an appropriate transitional remark. Avoid such weak transitions as: 'This next chart is supposed to explain...'
6. Keep the action moving. Don't tarry with any of the charts longer than necessary to make your point, unless someone from the audience has a pertinent question. You can always turn back to specific charts during a question-answer period.
7. After you cover each chart, summarize the main point. The last chart in the series might be a listing of each of the key points from the preceding charts.[2]

Projected Visuals

Recent technology has made projected visuals useful as visual aids. Since a projected image continues to have appeal to viewers, interest is immediately obtained.

Present-day projection devices are relatively small and light weight—and thus are easily stored and transported. The major disadvantage of projected visuals is that special equipment is required for showing them and, in most cases, for producing the visuals. Some projected visuals, such as those used on an overhead projector, may be produced by simply writing on clear plastic with a wax pencil. Others, like sound film, require expensive sound cameras and other specialized equipment.

There are three types of projected visuals that can be used easily at meetings:

Slides

Two-by-two color slides are a versatile and easily used visual. Equipment is widely available for showing slides, and many individuals have cameras capable of taking slide pictures.

Producing slides is quite inexpensive. One of their prime advantages is they can be used to portray local situations. For example, a church adult education group studying inner-city conditions can be shown slides taken by some member of the group. A few carefully chosen slides are worth more than any amount of words to describe the conditions in the inner-city community.

Slides are a flexible visual medium. You can use the same slides for many purposes by simply rearranging their order. There is no imposed time restriction either. Your group can examine some slides at length and spend little time on others.

One disadvantage for slides is the requirement for a semi-darkened room.

Some suggestions for making a slide presentation are:
1. Edit the slides beforehand to make sure you have the right ones and they are all in proper sequence, with none upside down or wrong way around.
2. Limit the number of slides to the time available. Usually, you can figure on 15 to 20 seconds for each slide; some will take less.
3. Rehearse the entire presentation. Make any changes or notes beforehand. Make sure the slides are clean, since a big fingerprint or big black specks cannot fail to deglamorize your presentation.
4. Set up a lighted lectern so that you can read your notes as you make your presentation.
5. Use a remote control projector or an assistant to change the slides so that you will be able to face the audience as much as possible.

6. Tell the audience a little of your total presentation before you get started. Then lead somewhat into each new slide before you flash it. In this way, you prepare the audience for what is coming and make it a little more intense.
7. Never show slides after lunch, because you will come into competition with the effects of a full stomach working in a darkened room! The best time for slides is right after the coffee break.
8. Do not mix color with black-and-white. A different focus is required for each.
9. Change your pace from time to time during the presentation. This will help keep the audience on its toes. Make the first few slides a little on the slow and steady side. Then, if the subject matter permits, speed up a little for a few slides.[3]

Overhead Projector

The overhead projector is one of the most versatile types of projection equipment available. It basically works on the same principle as the slide projector: a light shines through a transparency and a lens projects the image on the screen. But the transparencies are much larger than slides, often $8\frac{1}{2}$ x 11 inches.

When using the overhead projector, the speaker stands behind the projector and faces his audience, with the screen behind him. Another advantage of this type of projector is that the room lights may be left on. Because the transparencies are simply placed on the horizontal stage, the speaker can operate the projector. The transparencies are large enough so the speaker, with a wax pencil, can write on the transparency as he talks. This equipment can thus be used in much the same manner as the chalkboard, with the added advantage that the speaker does not need to turn his back on the audience.

Motion Picture

There may be times to use a motion picture as a visual aid in your group deliberations. One of the main advantages of the motion picture is it combines visuals with the spoken work. When a process that involves motion is to be explained, it has a decided advantage. Because a motion picture can combine color, motion, and sound, it has a high interest factor.

There are many disadvantages to using films at group meetings. It is often extremely difficult to obtain a film for the purpose you have in mind. Some films may come close, but because you don't have flexibility you must accept the film or not accept it. You cannot rearrange the content as you can with slides and other forms of visualization.

Another decided disadvantage is the room must be darkened, which makes it difficult for viewers to take notes. Also, the equipment is heavy and difficult to transport and requires an experienced operator.

10

The Congregational Business Meeting

In addition to the many small-group meetings that churches hold, each year there are one or more business meetings to which the entire congregation is invited. Much of the material in other chapters of this book applies to the congregational business meeting, but some dimensions of a large group business meeting require special attention.

Let's start with the basic question: what's the purpose of congregational business meetings, why hold them? Most church constitutions require a minimum of one congregational annual meeting to approve budgets, elect officers, and hear pastors' reports. There are some additional concerns that usually require congregational meetings—approving building plans, calling a new pastor, and so on.

Another purpose, although it doesn't relate directly to matters of business, is the opportunity for the congregation to get together for fellowship.

PLANNING

Agenda Building

It's essential that the agenda for a congregational meeting be carefully planned. Most annual meetings have certain routine agenda items that must be included:

discussion of the budget, election of officers, reports from the various church committees, pastor's report, approval of minutes of last annual meeting, and the treasurer's report.

The second category includes agenda items which would be classed as new business. Items for new business come from the church council, from the pastor, and from the various church committees and organizations. For example, new business items may be: Should we remodel the parsonage or help the pastor in buying a house of his own? or Should we hire a part time educational director for the church?

Whoever moderates the meeting—usually it's the president of the congregation—is responsible for getting the agenda together, but with the assistance of other church officers. In planning the agenda, some attention must be paid to the amount of time each agenda item will take. Long business meetings are often not productive. Carefully planning the agenda and budgeting time, at least tentatively, for each agenda item can help accomplish more in less time.

Preparation of the Membership

Sometimes the congregation is overlooked in the planning of business meetings. At least a week before the congregational meeting each member should receive a copy of the meeting agenda and a description of the issues that will be discussed. Much time at the annual meeting can be saved if various committee reports are distributed to the membership before the meeting. Then the committee moderator need only summarize the reports at the meeting and answer questions.

It's particularly important that background information on important questions be provided the membership before the meeting. Members can think about the issues before the meeting, and some will dig out additional information on an issue in which they have a particular interest.

Planning for Involvement

It's the moderator's responsibility to make certain that everyone who has a role in the meeting—those giving reports, those who will present background information on issues, and so on—are prepared. Each person should know before the meeting how much time he will have for his presentation.

Special Arrangements

Nothing should be taken for granted. The meeting room should be planned. Will people sit around tables or sit in straight rows? Will there be a podium for the moderator? Is it necessary to use a microphone?

If visual aids are planned, details should be checked. Who will get the equipment there? Who will operate a projector if one is being used?

Who will make the charts for the budget presentation? If it's assumed the treasurer will do it, does he know that?

If an outside speaker is planned, who is responsible for contacting this person? Who will greet him when he arrives? Does the moderator have information he can use for introducing the speaker? Does the speaker know exactly what's expected of him—the topic he's been assigned, the amount of time he has for speaking? Does the speaker need some audiovisual equipment? Who will be responsible for it?

The moderator should also arrange for a parliamentarian, someone who knows parliamentary procedure, to be at the meeting and decide on questions of rules.

CONDUCTING THE MEETING

Order of Business

Following is a more or less standard order of business that is often used at church business meetings. It is pos-

sible to vary the order, however, and still have a very successful meeting.
1. Call to order
2. Prayer
3. Minutes of last annual meeting (It usually saves time if these can be mailed to members before the meeting.)
4. Reports
   a. Treasurer's report
   b. Reports of standing committees, such as:
      1) Youth education
      2) Adult education
      3) Stewardship
      4) Life and growth
      5) Worship and music
      6) Buildings and grounds
   c. Reports of special committees, such as nominating committee
5. Unfinished business (items that may have been tabled at the last annual meeting)
6. New business (Here is where the agenda of special items to be considered are offered.)
7. Open forum (An opportunity for members to express their concerns or ask questions about anything relating to the church's activities)
8. Closing Prayer
9. Adjournment

If a speaker is part of the annual meeting, he may be on the program before the business meeting commences, he may be on after the new business, or he may be on after the business meeting is adjourned.

Starting on Time

The business meeting moderator has the problem of getting the meeting started on time. Starting 15 or 20 minutes late can steal valuable time away from discussion, limit the time for a speaker, and cause the meeting to last longer than it should.

What are some things that can be done to help get your business meeting started on time?

1. *Announce the starting time.* In all the publicity for the meeting say that it will start promptly. Make sure the time for the meeting is in bold type on the announcement.
2. *Start on time.* If people are accustomed to business meetings starting 15 minutes to a half hour late, they won't bother to get there on time.
3. *Have the speaker first.* One technique some congregations use, if they have a speaker at their annual meeting, is to put the speaker on the program first.
4. *Have a program before the business meeting.* Some congregations have a light supper at the church before the annual meeting. The business meeting starts exactly on time since the people are already there.
5. *Stimulate interest.* Reward those that come early by having various displays of church materials or exhibits, available for the early comers to view. For example, there might be a display of the Sunday school materials used, and the older youth could construct an exhibit that portrays some of their activities. There could be a display with materials explaining the activities of the national church office.

Parliamentary Procedure

Earlier we said that parliamentary procedure could bog down a small decision-making group. But for the large group, such as a congregational business meeting, parliamentary procedure is essential. Parliamentary procedure is based on two assumptions: the majority will rule, and the rights of the minority must be respected—all points of view must be heard.

Following is some basic information about parliamentary procedure. Refer to *Robert's Rules of Order* for a more comprehensive discussion.[1]

QUORUM. The number of people that must be present at a meeting before business can be transacted. For some churches, a quorum is the group of people that attend a business meeting. For other churches, the by-laws of the constitution may indicate that a quorum for a business meeting is five percent of the confirmed members of the church. That is, if the church has 500 confirmed members, then at least 25 people must be present at all congregation business meetings before business can be transacted. There are both advantages and disadvantages to having an established quorum. Without an established quorum an extremely small group of people, whoever happens to come to the meetings, can make decisions affecting the entire congregation. But if the annual business meeting falls on a night when the weather is bad, there may not be enough people able to get to the meeting to form a quorum.

MOTION. A request for action. When someone makes a motion he wants something to happen. The procedure for making and acting on motions is:

1. The person wishing to make a motion is recognized by the moderator.
2. The person states his motion: "I move that . . ."
3. Another person seconds that motion by saying: "I second that motion."
4. The moderator repeats the motion, in some instances helping the mover rephrase the motion so it is clear. Before repeating the motion the moderator will usually say, "It has been moved and seconded that . . ."
5. The group discusses the motion. The person making the motion is usually given the first opportunity to speak on the motion. Anytime before the vote is called for, the person making a motion may with-

draw it. Anyone may also amend the motion *(see below)*.

6. The vote is called for. The moderator will usually say, "Are you ready for the question?" Then he will again repeat the motion. Someone in the audience may also ask for the question, or they may move the previous question, which is a motion to close debate and bring the question to a vote.

7. The vote is taken. Usually it is a voice vote with the moderator saying, "All in favor of the motion signify by saying aye, opposed no." If the outcome of the voice vote is not obvious, the moderator may ask for the aye's to stand, and then the no's to stand, or he may ask first the aye's and then the no's to raise their hands. Most motions require a majority vote, but some require a 2/3 majority. Examples of motions requiring a 2/3 majority are those to close nominations and motions to close debate on a motion.

AMENDMENT TO A MOTION. When someone wishes to modify a motion on the floor, he moves to amend it. The motion to amend must be seconded, and when it is seconded the discussion switches from the main motion to the amendment. A simple majority vote is necessary for an amendment to pass. If the amendment passes, then the discussion switches back to the main motion, as it is now amended. If the amendment loses, the discussion switches back to the main motion as it was before the amendment was offered.

AMENDMENT TO AN AMENDMENT. This occurs when someone wishes to modify an amendment. The amendment to the amendment must be seconded and the discussion switches to the amendment to the amendment. No further amendment is permissible.

MOVING THE PREVIOUS QUESTION. If someone wishes to stop the discussion on a motion, he may say, "I move the previous question." Or he may say, using language we use today, "I move we vote on the motion before us, without anymore discussion." The motion requires a two-thirds vote to pass. When a motion to move the previous question has passed, the group must then vote on the motion before the meeting.

NOMINATIONS. Most churches follow the procedure of a nominating committee that develops a slate of officers that is presented to the church body. When the nominees offered by the committee are presented at the business meeting, the nominations must also be opened to the entire group.

To make a nomination, a person need not be recognized by the moderator. And no second is required for a nomination. No one can nominate more than one person for a given office. When there are no further nominations coming from the floor, the moderator may say, "Are there further nominations for the office?" If there are none, the moderator may declare the nominations closed without waiting for a motion from the floor. Someone may also move that the nominations be closed. This requires a second and a 2/3 majority to pass.

POINT OF ORDER. When anyone at a business meeting feels a rule is being violated, he has the right to stand and say "point of order," without being recognized by the moderator. This action does not require a second and is not debatable. Point of order should only be used when someone's rights are being infringed or there is a major rule violation. The point of order can be abused when it is used to slow down a meeting by raising questions about minor irregularities that have little effect on the transaction of business.

When a person raises a point of order, the moderator asks him to state his point of order. Then the moderator rules either that a rule was or was not broken. The moderator may refer the issue to the parliamentarian for advice, before he declares his ruling.

For example, a motion to approve the church's budget has been made and seconded. The group is discussing various dimensions of the budget when someone starts to speak about an action of the pastor that this person did not approve of.

It is appropriate at this moment for someone to say, "Point of order." The moderator must recognize the point of order and the person speaking must stop. The moderator will ask, "What is your point of order?" The response may be, "This person is not talking to the motion at hand, the church budget."

The moderator will rule on the point of order and may say, "The point of order is well taken. Would you please be seated. Perhaps you'll want to bring up your concern later."

THE MEETING MODERATOR

1. Is impartial. Trys to balance contributions by those for and against an issue. Doesn't vote unless there's a tie.

2. Encourages contributions from the group, controls the amount of talking he personally does.

3. Has the meeting planned. Knows what's supposed to happen next.

4. Keeps the meeting on schedule as much as possible without denying people the opportunity to contribute. Starts the meeting on time, ends on time.

5. Prevents the meeting from being interrupted by people who have something to say, but not about the issue being discussed. Encourages these people to make their comments during the open forum period at the end of the meeting.

6. Tries to be as informal as possible, yet enforces the rules of parliamentary procedure.

7. When necessary, acts as translator. He may, with the consent of the mover, improve a badly worded motion.

8. Avoids drawing attention to himself by trying to be

a comic, although at times a well-told story may help to relieve many tensions.

9. Never publically criticizes comments made by congregational members at the meeting.

10. Refers difficult questions of parliamentary procedure to the parliamentarian.

11

Be a Better Speaker

People who work with groups are often asked to give speeches. Particularly is this true of group leaders—committee moderators, council presidents, and the like. Often members of a group may be asked to present a report of their group's activities to another group, or at times to the entire congregation. So speech-making skills become valuable.

Public speaking, like almost everything else people do, can be learned. The best speakers were not born with that ability; they acquired it through hard work and practice. Following are some tips that may be useful as you plan and give speeches.

PLANNING A SPEECH

When planning a talk you must consider three elements: (1) the purpose of the talk, (2) the audience, and (3) the occasion.

Know the Purpose of the Speech

No one should give a talk without some specific purpose in mind. In general there are three purposes:

1. To inform
2. To persuade
3. To entertain

The three purposes are closely related. If the purpose

of your talk is to persuade your audience to do something, you'll probably need to inform them first, and to keep your talk interesting you may do some entertaining.

Most of the speeches you'll give will likely be designed either to inform or persuade. Some speakers fall into the trap of believing their most important purpose is to entertain their audience; consequently they neither inform nor persuade.

If you are a committee moderator, one of your first assignments will be to give opening remarks at the first meeting of your committee. The primary purpose of that speech is to inform, though you may do some entertaining to accomplish that purpose. You'll tell the members the purpose of the committee and the ground rules: starting time, ending time, the resources your committee has available, and so on. That's one kind of speech, though it may only be five or 10 minutes long.

You may also be asked to present the decision of your committee to the entire congregation for their action. For example, you may be moderator of a committee to draft a revised constitution for your church. To get the constitution approved, the entire congregation must act on your committee's recommendations. You'll have to explain to the entire congregation the actions of your committee *(you inform them)* and then you'll indicate why you think your committee's work should be accepted by the entire congregation *(you persuade them)*.

Know Your Audience

Before you speak to a group, learn as much as you can about it. How large is the group? What are their ages? How much do they already know about the subject you'll be presenting?

Of course, if you're speaking to your own committee or to your congregation, you already know these answers. But you may be asked to speak to a group outside your church. Where do you get information about a group? The first source is from the person who asked you to speak. He should be able to give you most of the answers you need. You can also learn much about a group by arriving at your assigned speaking place in time to visit with the people before their meeting starts. You may revise some of your speech on the basis of what you learn from these conversations before the meeting.

When studying the audience, it's well to remember that most people want a subject presented to them in terms of *their* knowledge, experience and interest rather than in terms of *your* knowledge, experience, and interest. So it's imperative to learn as much as possible about your audience and develop your talk accordingly.

Know the Occasion

Will your talk follow a series of talks? Will it be a part of a business meeting? Are you first on the program after a dinner? Are you last on the program after a busy evening? Is this a recognition night?

Each of these situations may cause you to make some minor modifications in your speech. If your talk immediately follows a dinner, you may want the group to stand and stretch before you start. If your talk is at the end of a long evening, you may have to pare it down. If the meeting is a celebration, you'll want to adjust your talk to that mood.

The purpose of your talk must fit the occasion. If you're unfamiliar with the meeting place for the group, find out about it. How will the group be seated—in rows of chairs, or around tables, at a long banquet table? Will you be using a microphone? Will there be a lectern? If you plan to use visual aids, who is providing the equipment?

The more you can learn about the occasion and the setting, the better you can plan your speech.

WRITING YOUR SPEECH

Now for the difficult part—actually writing the speech. You have decided on the purpose of your talk and you know the audience and the occasion, but what will you say? And how will you organize what you have to say?

Don't wait until the time to deliver your talk to answer these questions. Effective speeches are planned, they don't just happen. Occasionally, you'll be asked to give off-the-cuff talks to groups, and sometimes you may be quite effective. But how often have you over-emphasized something or forgotten an important point when you had to give an impromptu talk?

In the majority of situations you'll have ample time to plan your talk. Use this time to advantage.

There are three parts to most talks: an introduction, a body, and a conclusion. When you start your talk, you warm up your audience and tell them what you are going to say—the *introduction*. You say what you have to say—the *body*. And you tell them again what you have said—the *conclusion*. Let's look at each segment.

The introduction. Before you launch into your main points, you must help the audience get used to you and your way of speaking. Some speakers use the first few minutes to tell a story that's relevant to the situation. This isn't necessary, but if you're a good storyteller it can be an effective ice breaker. If you get to the meeting early, you may hear some comments that you can use in your introductory remarks. You may have overheard two people talking about speakers who talk too long. In your initial remarks you might say, "I know the rules of the game for this group. I've jotted a note to myself that I better not be a long-winded speaker. So I'm taking off my watch and putting it here in front of me." You have given your audience the feeling that you're one of them. Also, before getting into the body of your talk, you need to warm up the audience to the topic you have been assigned. Tell them in brief outline form what you'll be talking about.

For example, let's assume you are moderator of your church's music committee and another church invites you to speak on the activities of your committee for the past year. After a few warm-up statements you might say, "Tonight I want to share with you what our committee has done with the music program at our church, what the choir is doing, how young people are involved, and how we use music during the worship services."

The audience now knows the framework in which you will operate and is prepared to hear the details of each of the topics you mentioned.

Apologizing is an error that many speakers make in the introduction of their talk. Some apologize for almost everything—for being there, for being unprepared, for being a poor choice to talk on the subject, or for being a poor speaker. Even though some of the above may be true, it's better for the audience to find out for itself. And if it's true you're unprepared to speak, then you probably shouldn't be there.

The body of your speech is where you develop the facts, where you present the information within the framework you outlined in your introduction. In the body of the talk you must keep your audience interested and moving with you from one major point to another. To do this you must balance facts with examples. You must balance statistics with word pictures and perhaps with visuals.

Anecdotes can illustrate something that is abstract and not quickly understood by the audience. For example, I was speaking to a group about adult resistance to change, that it was human nature to be hesitant about changing the way we do things. This statement was met with some blank stares from the audience. I went on to explain that I usually drive to work on the same street every day and that one day the street was closed for repairs. I had to find a different way. But which way should

I go, which alternate route would have the least traffic and yet not take so long that I would be late for work? I was unhappy about making a change. I knew every chuck hole on the route I was used to traveling. As a result of the roadblock I found a way to work that was shorter and had less traffic than the way I had traveled for many years. Because I was fearful of change, I didn't look for a better way until I was forced.

After relating the anecdote, the group seemed to understand. "Oh, that's what he means by resistance to change." Some heads were nodding to indicate understanding.

It's during the body of the talk that you'll make the major inroads toward accomplishing the purpose of your talk, a purpose that you should always have clearly in mind as you speak.

When you've covered the major points of your talk and elaborated sufficiently on each of them, don't stop, leaving your audience in mid-air. Move into your *conclusion,* summarizing what you've said and indicating again what action people are expected to take, if you're giving a speech to persuade. Don't end your speech by apologizing for how long you talked or thank the audience for listening to you. And don't be anticlimactic. When you have finished with your conclusion, sit down.

As you think through what you plan to include in each of the three segments of your talk, jot down the main elements. By doing this you're developing a written outline for your talk. With the outline on paper, fill in the blank spaces with the facts, figures, and anecdotes needed to accomplish your purpose.

Even though you plan to deliver your talk from notes, it's helpful to write out the talk as you plan to give it. Write as you talk. The discipline of writing the entire speech helps clarify the wording for segments of the talk that you may find difficult if you only prepare notes.

Writing out the talk also helps you get a better idea

of the time it will take to deliver a speech. You know the amount of time you've been assigned, and with simple mathematics you can match the material to the time assigned. An ordinary typewritten page, double-spaced, contains about 250 words. With average rate of delivery, about 125 words per minute, each page of copy will take about two minutes of speaking time.

Once you've written your speech and have revised it to the form in which you will deliver it, prepare the notes you'll use in presenting the speech. Here's where you need to make a decision: will you use notes when delivering your talk or will you read the manuscript? This will depend a great deal on you, your manner of speaking, and the occasion. If the occasion is a formal one, and the nature of your talk is such that it's important that your words be as you have written them, then you may want to read your speech. But if it's an informal situation, as most are, you probably don't want to read your speech.

When preparing notes, place them on full-size paper, double-spaced typing. Having notes on notecards may seem like a good idea, until the notecards are accidently shuffled, or dropped and become mixed. The speaker then is forced to reshuffle and may lose the audience in the process.

Your preparation isn't complete with writing the speech and preparing notes. You need to practice delivering the talk. One of the best ways for some people to practice is to tape record the speech while standing in front of a mirror. You can watch your delivery, observe if your gestures look natural and note any other flaws, such as your delivery stance. The recorder will give you the opportunity to play back your talk and allow revision of passages that look correct on paper, but need to be changed when you hear them spoken. These practice sessions are a good check on the time required to deliver the speech too.

If you can get a friend or your spouse to listen to your speech, you may get feedback that can help you improve your presentation.

GIVING THE SPEECH

If you have given few speeches, one of your first concerns is probably stage fright. The thought of standing before a group of people and speaking may terrify you. If it's any consolation, you're not alone. Stage fright is experienced by nearly everyone who gives speeches. Good speakers use it to advantage. They feel that the nervousness they experience before speaking helps to sharpen them, helps them to be more aware of their audience and perceptive to how the audience is receiving them.

There are some techniques to help control nervousness and use it to advantage. Good preparation before your speech is the best controller of stage fright. The feeling of confidence that comes from knowing exactly what you are going to say and how you will say it will eliminate most of the prespeaking jitters.

Just before you stand to speak, take a deep breath. This often helps to control the feeling of inadequacy that you may have. And when you start to speak, deliver the first lines more slowly and deliberately, than your normal speaking rate. If you do this, the sound of your voice will help restore your confidence and the remainder of your talk will flow easily and naturally.

There are no quick cures for stage fright. But through experience you acquire speaking confidence so you can more easily control it. But don't try to eliminate stage fright completely; if you succeed you'll be a dull speaker.

Eye Contact

An error many beginning speakers make is talking to their notes. Your assignment is talking to your audience, not your notes. Each person in the audience likes to believe that you're talking personally to him. You accomplish this feeling of one-to-one communication by looking directly at people when you speak. Shift your gaze from person to person, looking directly at each person as you talk to him. Then shift your gaze to another and repeat the process. You not only create the feeling of talking directly to the audience, but you're able to determine how the audience is reacting to your presentation by their facial expressions. If you notice that some of the audience looks bored, you can interject an anecdote to perk them up. Some may appear not to understand what you are saying; take the clue and rephrase what you have said to achieve better understanding. The experienced speaker is able to "read" an audience as he speaks to them and to adjust his remarks accordingly.

Some beginning speakers—unfortunately some experienced speakers—feel they can accomplish eye contact by staring at some fixed object in the back of the room or by staring at one or two people throughout the talk. This procedure accomplishes little more than if you spend your time staring at your notes.

Using Notes

If you feel you must read your speech, then do it; but don't apologize. Although it may seem to the beginner that reading a speech is easier than talking from notes, the opposite is true. It's extremely difficult to read a speech and keep the delivery interesting. It requires much more preparation and practice than speaking from notes.

The person who reads his speech must spend more time looking at his manuscript and thus isn't able to maintain the most efficient eye contact. Even if you read your speech, you must force yourself to look at the audience as often as possible.

When you read, try to let the words flow from the page as you would normally speak them. Avoid the rut of allowing your voice to become a droning monotone that lulls everyone to sleep.

And whether you use notes or a complete manuscript, leave the printed material on the lectern. Waving your notes to the audience only creates a distraction; it doesn't help to emphasize major points.

Distracting Mannerisms

Some speakers pace back and forth behind the lectern. Others tug on their ears, rub their stomachs, twist paper clips, brush back their hair, button and unbutton their coats. Other speakers repeatedly say "ah," "and ah," or "you know." All of these mannerisms detract from what you have to say. Some detract so much that those who listen to you aren't interested in what you're saying, but are counting the number of times you put your hands in your pockets or say "you know."

Practicing in front of a mirror, using a tape recorder, or having a friend listen to your talk will help to eliminate many of these detracting mannerisms—mannerisms that many speakers don't even know they have.

Improper use of a microphone can be a distraction. If you are required to use a mike, make certain it is adjusted for you and then forget it. The microphone should be about six inches from your mouth. Do not tap on it with a pencil or try to move it up and down as you speak. And because you have a mike, don't feel you can whisper. Speak as you would without a mike, in a voice that is slightly louder than your normal person-to-person voice.

Many speakers ask "What do I do with my hands? When I start speaking they feel like blocks of wood hanging on the ends of my arms."

Let them hang naturally at your sides. This will look perfectly normal to your audience even though it doesn't to you. Or rest your hands on the lectern; don't grasp the lectern as if it were going to try to escape.

Introducing Speakers

One task you'll often get is introducing speakers, especially if your group uses resource people. There are some principles to follow that will make this job easier for you and easier for the speaker.

When introducing a speaker, remember that he is the speaker and you're introducing him. Your job is not to give a speech. Yet how often have you heard an introduction that was 15 minutes or even longer?

Your job is to arouse curiosity about the speaker and his job. To do this tell something about the speaker, such as who he is, where he's from, his present position, and the experiences he has that qualify him to speak on the assigned topic. Avoid such trite phrases as "It's an honor and a privilege . . . ," "I give you . . . ," or "The speaker today needs no introduction . . ." If the speaker doesn't need an introduction, why are you introducing him?

Indicate why you have invited this speaker to the meeting. Everyone may not know.

Following are some general guidelines for introducing speakers:

1. Indicate the speaker's name at the beginning of the introduction and again just before he starts speaking.

2. Don't tell jokes about the speaker that may embarrass him.

3. Never apologize for a speaker who is a substitute for the one you had hoped to get.

4. Don't talk about yourself. The group is interested in the speaker.

5. Don't launch into such a complete description of the speaker's talk that you take away from his presentation.

6. Don't tell your group what a fine speaker this person is.

7. Don't give his complete biography; select those items that seem most appropriate for the occasion.

8. Discuss the introduction with the speaker to be sure it is correct and acceptable.

9. Write out what you plan to say before the meeting. This will help prevent embarrassing errors that often occur with the pressure of the meeting. Don't be like the moderator who was introducing County Judge John Van Loon to his group. The introduction came out "And now, John Van Judge, our County Loon."

10. Be brief.

12

How Are We Doing?

Occasionally we need to stop, step back, and look at our meetings. We need to ask, how are we doing? An evaluation of meetings can help us identify areas of weakness and make plans for improving our meetings.

To make future plans, a group must know where it has been and where it is at the present time. A group also needs to know if the procedures it is using are working and are being accepted by the membership.

To evaluate a meeting, you must know what you want to evaluate and why. Some questions you might answer are:

1. Has the group accomplished its purpose?
2. Are the participants satisfied with the arrangements, meeting time, etc?
3. Are the participants satisfied with how the group deals with problems?
4. Are the participants satisfied with their opportunities to participate and interact with each other?

What Is Evaluated?

Two broad areas for evaluating a group meeting are:

1. How was the meeting planned and conducted?
2. What were the outcomes of the meeting?

For instance, if you are moderator of your church's financial committee and have held a budget preparation meeting, you might evaluate:

—Preparations for the meeting
—Involvement of members at the meeting
—Utilization of the decision-making process
—Use of visual aids
—Follow-up of the meeting

To evaluate each of those items, you must know what is acceptable. For example, to evaluate involvement of members at a meeting, you may decide that acceptable involvement is when all or nearly all of the members participate in the discussion at one time or another. With that standard of what's acceptable, you need to find out what the level of involvement was and compare it to the standard.

Besides knowing how well the meeting was planned and conducted, you will likely want to know what the meeting accomplished. To evaluate a meeting's accomplishments, you must know the group's purposes. If one of the purposes of the financial committee was to develop a written budget, then a simple evaluation question to ask is "Was a written budget prepared?" Of course the quality dimension of the meeting's output must also be considered. Questions like the following must be asked: Will the budget be understandable to the congregational members? Is the budget accurately developed? and Is the budget realistic when compared to anticipated congregational giving?

Some Evaluation Approaches

1. Post-meeting reaction sheets. Two examples of these are included at the end of this chapter. Of course each person that responds has his own standards against which he makes a judgment.

2. Group discussion. At the end of a meeting, or during a meeting say after or just before a break, the group may discuss for a few minutes how things are going.

3. Pre-selected participants in the group can be asked

to meet with other participants and report to the entire group what they learned about what the group was accomplishing and the suitability of the approaches used.

4. One or two participants can be asked before the meeting to observe what's happening, and then at the end of the meeting share what they've seen and heard.

When to Evaluate

In a sense, a group leader evaluates his group constantly. He is concerned about how the meetings are being conducted and whether the group is accomplishing its purposes.

But to get more detailed information, an end-of-meeting or one of the other evaluation approaches mentioned above may be used periodically. If your group is a committee that meets monthly, you may want the committee to look at itself more systematically once or twice a year.

Most groups that meet on a continuing basis have established times when they review their purposes for the coming year. This is the obvious time to review past accomplishments, as well as review the approaches the committee has used. With this approach, evaluation is not viewed as something "tacked on" to already full meeting agendas, but is an integral part of the group's operation.

Leader Evaluation

Occasionally, the leader may want to look at himself and his methods of operating. A check-sheet is included at the end of this chapter for that purpose.

END-OF-MEETING REACTION FORM

1. This meeting was: good _____ fair _____ poor _____
2. What did you expect would be accomplished at this meeting?
3. What was accomplished at this meeting?
4. What questions were not answered?
5. How could the meeting have been improved?

END-OF-MEETING REACTION FORM

1. How did you feel about this meeting? *(check)*
   Terrible ____ Poor ____ So-So ____ Good ____
   Excellent ____
2. What were the meeting's strengths?
3. What were the weaknesses?
4. What improvements do you suggest?

END-OF-MEETING EVALUATION[1]

Small Group Discussion

(Please circle your rating)	Low		Rating		High
1. How satisfied were you with this session?	1	2	3	4	5
2. To what extent did you feel comfortable in the group?	1	2	3	4	5
3. To what extent do you know the group members?	1	2	3	4	5
4. To what extent were your personal objectives met?	1	2	3	4	5
5. To what extent did you contribute to the discussion?	1	2	3	4	5
6. To what extent did the group stay on the assigned topic?	1	2	3	4	5
7. I would rate the group leader.	1	2	3	4	5

Suggestions:

END-OF-MEETING SUGGESTION SLIP[2]

What is your over-all rating of today's meeting for each of the items? Please circle appropriate number.

	Very Low	Low	Ave.	High	Very High
1. Physical arrangement and comfort	1	2	3	4	5
2. Orientation	1	2	3	4	5
3. Group atmosphere	1	2	3	4	5
4. Interest and motivation	1	2	3	4	5
5. Participation	1	2	3	4	5
6. Productiveness	1	2	3	4	5
7. Choice of methods	1	2	3	4	5

CHECK LIST FOR GROUP LEADER

Before the Meeting

_____ 1. Were you prepared for the meeting?
_____ 2. Did you have the equipment you needed?
_____ 3. Was the meeting place the best you could provide?
_____ 4. Were the members properly notified?
_____ 5. Did you have a prepared agenda?
_____ 6. Were your introductory remarks carefully planned?

Beginning of the Meeting

_____ 1. Were the committee members introduced to each other?
_____ 2. Did you adhere to the stated starting time?
_____ 3. Did everyone know the purpose of the meeting?
_____ 4. Was the topic for discussion clearly introduced?

Body of the Meeting

_____ 1. Did the committee enter readily into the discussion?
_____ 2. Did you follow the decision-making process?
_____ 3. Was there sufficient information for effective decision making?
_____ 4. Did everyone understand the problems discussed?
_____ 5. Did the committee stay on the subject?
_____ 6. Did the committee members enter readily into the discussion?
_____ 7. Were you able to recognize roles played by committee members?
_____ 8. Were you able to handle "problem" members?
_____ 9. Did you provide a break if the meeting was longer than two hours?
_____ 10. Were committee minutes kept?
_____ 11. Was variety used in presenting material to committee members?
_____ 12. Were visual materials used at the meeting for added interest and understanding?

Close of the Meeting

_____ 1. Was the meeting atmosphere conducive to free discussion?
_____ 2. Did you reach conclusions?
_____ 3. Did you provide for meeting follow-up?
_____ 4. Did you adhere to an established ending time?
_____ 5. Did you do most of the talking at the meeting?
_____ 6. Did the committee waste time?
_____ 7. Was there considerable post-meeting discussion?
_____ 8. Were most or all of the members in attendance?

Notes

CHAPTER 1

1. Norman R. F. Maier, *Problem Solving and Creativity,* (Belmont, California: Brooks/Cole Publishing Co., 1970), pp. 325-326.

CHAPTER 2

1. Sheldon G. Lowery, *Committees . . . A Key to Group Leadership,* North Central Regional Extension Publication No. 18 (East Lansing, Michigan: Michigan State University, 1965), p. 4.
2. *Ibid.*

CHAPTER 3

1. Sheldon G. Lowery, *Committees . . . A Key to Group Leadership,* North Central Regional Extension Publication No. 18, (East Lansing, Michigan: Michigan State University, 1965), p. 3.
2. See Leslie E. This, *The Small Meeting Planner,* (Houston, Texas: Gulf Publishing Company, 1972), pp. 95-118 for a more detailed discussion of arrangements.

CHAPTER 4

1. Daniel I. Stufflebeam, et. al. *Educational Evaluation Decision Making,* (Itasca, Illinois: F. E. Peacock Publishers, Inc., 1971), pp. 81-84.

CHAPTER 5

1. Andre L. Delbecq and Andrew H. Van De Ven, "A Group Process Model for Problem Identification and Program Planning," *The Journal of Applied Behavioral Science*, Vol. 7, No. 4 (1971), pp. 466-492.
2. Norman R. F. Maier, *Problem-Solving, Discussions and Conferences*, (New York: McGraw-Hill Book Company, 1963), 103-115.
3. Norman R. F. Maier, *Problem Solving and Creativity*, (Belmont, California: Brooks/Cole Publishing Company, 1970), p. 277.
4. John K. Brilhart, *Effective Group Discussion* (Dubuque, Iowa: William C. Brown Company Publishers, 1967), p. 30.
5. *Ibid.*, pp. 31-32.
6. J. H. McPherson, "The People, the Problems and the Problem Solving Methods," *The Journal of Creative Behavior*, Vol. 2, No. 2, Spring, 1968.

CHAPTER 6

1. George M. Beal, Joe M. Bohlen and J. Neil Raudabaugh, *Leadership and Dynamic Group Action*, (Ames, Iowa: The Iowa State University Press, 1962), p. 107.

CHAPTER 7

1. Fred E. Fiedler, "Personality and Situational Determinants of Leadership Effectiveness," in Dorwin Cartwright and Alvin Zander, Group Dynamics, 3rd edition (New York: Harper and Row, Publishers, 1968), p. 362.
2. *Ibid.* p. 373.
3. *Ibid.* p. 372.
4. *Ibid.* p. 369.
5. Robert S. Cathcart and Larry A. Samovar, *Small Group Communication*, (Dubuque, Iowa: William C. Brown Company, Publishers, 1970), pp. 385-394.
6. *Ibid.* p. 391.
7. *Ibid.* p. 391.

CHAPTER 8

1. Paul Bergevin, Dwight Morris, and Robert M. Smith, *Adult Education Procedures* (New York: Seabury Press, 1963), p. 127.
2. *Ibid.*
3. *Ibid.*, pp. 129-130.
4. Eric Berne, *Games People Play* (New York: Grove Press, Inc., 1964).
5. Saville Sax and Sandra Hollander, *Reality Games* (New York: Macmillan Company, 1972).
6. Bergevin, Morris, and Smith, *Adult Education Procedures*, p. 137.

CHAPTER 9

1. B. Y. Auger, *How to Run Better Business Meetings* (St. Paul, Minnesota: Business Services Press, Visual Products Division, 3M Company, 1966), p. 44.
2. *Ibid.*, p. 49. Reprinted by permission of and copyrighted 1966 by Minnesota Mining and Manufacturing Company.
3. *Ibid.*, pp. 52-53. Reprinted by permission of and copyrighted 1966 and 1972 by Minnesota Mining and Manufacturing Company.

CHAPTER 10

1. Henry M. Robert, Sarah Corbin Robert, *Robert's Rules of Order—Newly Revised* (Glenview, Illinois: Scott, Foresman and Company, 1970).

CHAPTER 12

1. Jerold W. Apps, *How to Improve Adult Education in Your Church* (Minneapolis, Minnesota: Augsburg Publishing House, 1972), p. 86.
2. George M. Beal, Joe M. Bohlen, and J. Neil Raudabaugh *Leadership and Dynamic Group Action* (Ames, Iowa: The Iowa State University Press, 1962), p. 294.